Y0-BRJ-373

DATE DUE

FEB 21 1992			
MAY 17 1995 NOV 07 1995			
APR 26 2006			

DEMCO 38-297

RENNER
LEARNING RESOURCES CENTER
ELGIN COMMUNITY COLLEGE
ELGIN, ILLINOIS 60120

DRAMA IN PRACTICE

DRAMA IN PRACTICE

A handbook for students

Peter Spalding

RENNER LEARNING RESOURCE CENTER
ELGIN COMMUNITY COLLEGE
ELGIN, ILLINOIS 60123

MACMILLAN

© Peter Spalding 1985

All rights reserved. No reproduction, copy or transmission of this publication may be made without written permission.

No paragraph of this publication may be reproduced, copied or transmitted save with written permission or in accordance with the provisions of the Copyright Act 1956 (as amended).

Any person who does any unauthorised act in relation to this publication may be liable to criminal prosecution and civil claims for damages.

First published 1985

Published by
Higher and Further Education Division
MACMILLAN PUBLISHERS LTD
Houndmills, Basingstoke, Hampshire RG21 2XS
and London
Companies and representatives
throughout the world

Typeset by
Wessex Typesetters
Frome, Somerset

Printed in Hong Kong

British Library Cataloguing in Publication Data
Spalding, Peter
  Drama in practice.
  1. Theater—Production and direction
  I. Title
  792'.0232   PN2053

  ISBN 0–333–37430–4
  ISBN 0–333–37431–2 Pbk

RENNER LEARNING RESOURCE CENTER
ELGIN COMMUNITY COLLEGE
ELGIN, ILLINOIS 60123

792.0232
5739d

073950

Contents

Acknowledgements

The author and publishers wish to thank the following who have kindly given permission for the use of copyright material:

ACTAC (Theatrical & Cinematic) Ltd for extract from *Ibsen: Peer Gynt*, translated by Christopher Fry.

Associated Book Publishers Ltd for extract from *Bertold Brecht Poems*, edited by J Willett and R Manheim (Methuen 1981); and extract from *What the Butler Saw* (Methuen 1969).

J M Dent & Sons Ltd and Everyman's Library for extract from *Ghosts*, translated by J Farquharson Sharp (1969).

Elaine Greene Ltd on behalf of Arthur Miller for an extract from *Death of a Salesman*, published by Martin Secker and Warburg Ltd and Penguin Books Ltd, © 1949 by Arthur Miller.

Oxford University Press for extract from *The Bear* in Chekhov Short Plays translated by R Hingley (1968).

Every effort has been made to trace all the copyright holders but if any have been inadvertently overlooked the publishers will be pleased to make the necessary arrangements at the first opportunity.

List of Illustrations

The author and publishers are grateful to copyright holders for
permission to use photographs.

Introduction

This book is for the use of students of literature and drama, especially those preparing for examinations. Its aim is to provide practical techniques for the study of eight major plays. Two of these are by Shakespeare and the other six have been chosen from the works of Wilde, Chekhov, Ibsen, Miller, Brecht and Bond. Because this is a 'handbook' designed for use under workshop conditions it has certain structural features different from the usual study textbook. Students are asked to read this introduction carefully before starting work.

To those who question the need for a new kind of textbook it could be said that while private study and group discussion of texts remain essential it is also true that no playtext ever becomes a complete work of art until it is performed in front of an audience.

Many people would agree that the best way to get to know any play is to take an active part in a performance, but to mount a full-length production takes more time and costs more money than is often available in a school or college. In any case, the time and energy that student actors must expend in the sheer repetitive slog towards perfection could be better utilised in exploration and experiment. In short, continuous workshop experience may be better for students than public performance. The basic study technique is by means of *simulation*. Although the group is not intending to produce the play in actuality it works through most of the main procedures *as if* it intends to do so. This means that the student has to assume different functional roles according to circumstances.

Sometimes, he will be expected to think about the play as if he were a director trying to fathom the author's intentions in order to explain them to his actors or as a designer considering how to use the physical resources at his disposal to evoke an appropriate mood in an audience, but for most of the time students will be working together helping each other to improve their techniques to make them more worthy of the works they have chosen to study and subsequently applying those techniques to an interpretation of the plays.

It is hoped that students will feel free to use this book to suit the convenience of their particular studies. They will find that each chapter is divided into six modular units arranged in sequence parallel to the other chapters. It is therefore possible to read the book 'horizontally' as well as 'vertically' and it is not obligatory to begin at Chapter One. Having made his choice of play, the student is asked to work systematically through the chapter answering any questions that may be put to him and following up the suggestions for practical work. He will find that his attention is being called to units in other chapters. This usually provides an opportunity for further experience and practice. (For instance, the term 'improvisation' is used in many different ways. These are fully explored in **Unit 3** throughout the book.)

An indication of the contents of the modular units follows.

Unit 1   Barriers across the path

It must be admitted that classic plays are seldom easy to understand at a first reading. The very fact that every play in this book has become an examination text has tended to surround it with an atmosphere of anxiety, but it is true that every major playwright always creates a highly personal style and idiom, not always immediately understood by audiences in their own countries and at their own time. (Chekhov may seem difficult to us, but he also presented problems for Russian audiences in 1896!) Critics and commentators trying to be helpful sometimes obscure the play by giving students too much information about it. These introductory units offer the student practical ways of discovering the nature and content of the play itself within the context of its period and country of origin.

Unit 2   Preparing for the task

In these units, the student is called upon to think of himself as an actor concerned first with learning and then with improving his personal techniques. Relaxation, movement, speech and improvisation exercises are the main ingredients in the training of professional actors. It is recommended that students refer to **Unit 2** throughout the book in search of ideas which can be adapted to the purposes of the plays which interest them.

Unit 3   Exploring the background

These units are mainly concerned with improvisation. The most powerful tool at the disposal of any actor is his imagination without which techniques of speech and movement will remain sterile. The Russian director Stanislavsky, when producing Chekhov's plays for the first time, evolved a process of creative improvisation which became the foundation of the professional techniques in use today.

Unit 4   Characters and relationships

Great artists differ widely in the ways in which they may paint a portrait. So do great playwrights in the way that they depict their characters. Consequently actors must learn to adjust their techniques accordingly.

Unit 5   Rehearsing the scene

For each play, typical scenes are shown as they would be treated in rehearsal by an experienced director. While every director has a personal style most of them tend to follow a process from read-through and discussion to 'setting rehearsal' and then onwards through a series of rehearsals culminating in the performance. In this book there will be concentration upon particular sequences in the plays which may contain keys to the understanding of the main themes. It is hoped that students will also choose their own exemplar scenes and direct them for themselves.

Unit 6   Realisation

These units are not intended to give practical advice on the staging of the plays. There are already a large number of excellent books about design and stage-management. The aim is to examine the ways in which consideration of practical staging-problems can enlighten the study of text. Nobody can begin to answer the question 'What does this play mean?' unless he rephrases it to say, 'What does this play mean to me?' Such a question can never be answered by reference to a text nor by means of an essay or even a lecture.

The actor can answer it completely only by the manner in which he plays his part; the director, in the way in which his overall vision is expressed; the designer and the stage-manager, by the way in which they have combined artistic and technical skills. All these should come together to make a unified statement to the audience which, in effect, says, 'This is what this play means to us.' Too often in working theatre, professional as well as amateur, the various tasks have become so specialised that only the director can retain an overall vision. People who feel that they lack artistic talent or technical skills can still make valuable contributions to design. They need not be called upon to draw or paint, nor to set up lighting-gear, but they can take an active part in research. This would entail more than reference to books. It could include collecting samples of suitable materials for costume and set-dressing and likely stage properties. The student who uses this book is fortunate in that he does not have to specialise. At some time or other during the study of his chosen plays, he has the chance to fulfil every working role in the production.

The author hopes that his readers will accept the word 'actor' as including 'actress' and the pronoun 'he' as including 'she' where relevant.

1
'Hamlet' by William Shakespeare

First produced by the Lord Chamberlain's Men at the Globe in 1600 or 1601. First published in a pirated edition 1603 and in the 'good' quarto 1604. There had been an earlier play of the same title attributed to Thomas Kyd written in 1589, but it is now lost. Richard Burbage played the title role although 'a trifle fat and scant of breath', and there is a tradition that Shakespeare played the Ghost. References to the text of the play are to the New Penguin Edition, edited by T. J. B. Spenser, published by Penguin Books, 1980.

1.1. Barriers across the path

Why is it that this play, generally accepted as being the greatest play by our most respected writer, is so seldom produced by amateurs? What arguments can be advanced for and against producing it? To bring the discussion to life, assume characters resembling the different kinds of people likely to be members of the planning committee of a local dramatic society. To concentrate discussion upon the play itself, presume that there are sufficient talent and experience among the actors, that there are adequate stage resources and that there is plenty of money available. Nevertheless there is likely to be opposition. If you improvise this scene truly, then sooner or later someone is likely to say something like this: 'I don't think we should spend money on producing *Hamlet*. It's such a boring play.' Of course, if it is not well produced and acted *Hamlet* can be as boring as any other play. The question is, how can it be produced without boring the audience?

1

1a   The frontispiece for Rowe's edition. (1709).

● Prepare a summary of the action, using no more than two or three lines
for each of the (how many?) scenes in the (how many?) acts. It will save
time to divide into small groups, each concentrating upon one of the acts.

● Note what is *done* rather than what is *said*, and as briefly as possible. For
instance: 'Act One, Scene 1 – Three soldiers plus Horatio see a ghost.
They decide to tell Hamlet about it.'

When the plot lines are complete it might be fun to play them through as a
'dumbshow' as in Act Three, Scene 2. The result may appear both incredible
and ridiculous and not a bit like what most people expect of a great and noble
tragedy, but improbability did not bother Elizabethan audiences, and, in any

case, the audience at any play should never be given time to think about the plot as it happens.

Another criticism is that the play is too long. Played in its entirety *Hamlet* can last four hours or more, so the practical producer must cut the play drastically. The most usual way of cutting *Hamlet* is by a process of plot surgery. Minor characters such as Cornelius, Voltemand and others seldom appear these days. Fortinbras is also often dispensed with, although to do so alters the plot. Discuss which characters seem to be unnecessary to the main plot or consider how much of the plot that involves Fortinbras is really necessary.

'But', say the objectors, 'it is neither plot nor length that puts people off. It is the old-fashioned style. Plays are no longer written in blank verse and the English language has changed so much that it is difficult to follow what is being said.' Put this objection to the test by looking at the very first scene of the play.

Enter FRANCISCO *and* BARNARDO, *two sentinels*.

BARNARDO: Who's there?

FRANCISCO: Nay, answer me. Stand and unfold yourself.

BARNARDO: Long live the King!

FRANCISCO: Barnardo?

BARNARDO: He.

FRANCISCO: You come most carefully upon your hour.

BARNARDO: 'Tis now struck twelve. Get thee to bed, Francisco.

FRANCISCO: For this relief much thanks. 'Tis bitter cold,
　　And I am sick at heart.

BARNARDO: Have you had quiet guard?

FRANCISCO: Not a mouse stirring.

BARNARDO: Well, good night.
　　If you do meet Horatio and Marcellus,
　　The rivals of my watch, bid them make haste.

At first sight there is not much here that seems at all difficult. The lines are set out as verse, but the metre is irregular and follows the patterns of ordinary speech. 'Unfold yourself' may seem odd when we first read it, but the intention is obvious. Most directors would cut it and trust the actors to make sense of the scene without it. So far, the language does not seem to have changed much. Nobody has difficulty in understanding 'rivals' to mean 'partners', especially if the actor *thinks* this meaning as he speaks the word. When he enters, Marcellus uses a more educated turn of speech, with words such as 'entreated' and 'apparition' instead of 'asked' and 'ghost'. This tendency of Shakespeare to change gear from simple to more learned speech can be one cause of confusion for the readers, though less so for the listener and least of all for the member of a theatre audience who sees the action as well as hears the lines spoken. Notice that Marcellus speaks in a more

3

regular rhythm than the soldiers. At times, he uses the five-stress, ten-syllable line known as **iambic pentameter**.

It is not long before the playwright changes gear again and gives us lines that could be accepted as modern speech:

> It would be spoke to. . . .
> Speak to it, Horatio. . . .
> It is offended. . . .
> See, it stalks away.

This is all very clear and simple but it might become boring if it went on too long, so Shakespeare, knowing that variety is the spice of drama, goes into another gear change. Marcellus asks Horatio why Denmark is preparing for war, and gets an answer which tends to go on and on. This sort of exposition speech plays into the hands of the objectors. (See also Chapter 2.1.)

Fortunately, if Fortinbras is cut, so is much of the speech, but Horatio has his reward coming. Almost immediately there is one more change of gear:

> In the most high and palmy state of Rome,
> A little ere the mightiest Julius fell,
> The graves stood tenantless, and the sheeted dead
> Did squeak and gibber in the Roman streets;
> As stars with trains of fire and dews of blood,
> Disasters in the sun; and the moist star,
> Upon whose influence Neptune's empire stands,
> Was sick almost to doomsday with eclipse.

This speech is a wonderful compound of sound, sense and feeling. If anybody in the audience did not altogether follow the sense, he could pick up the feeling from the sound. A number of vivid pictures are presented to the mind's eye. If the actor who spoke it knew his job, then everybody listening would *see* those corpses rising from their graves, *hear* the squeaking and gibbering,*see* the stars with trains of fire rushing overhead and *feel* the dews of blood as the moon went into eclipse.

When the Ghost suddenly reappears, there is another change of gear. The words must be played with very careful timing worked out between all four actors on the stage. The Ghost must be terrifying. (Perhaps because it does nothing?) It does not answer Horatio, and it is through him that the audience learn to be frightened of the ghost.

● Form small groups to prepare this part of the scene as a radio play from the beginning of Horatio's speech quoted above and ending with the exit of the Ghost. Use no music or special effects, but concentrate on creating the atmosphere by the way in which the words are spoken. The Ghost is silent throughout. Aim to make him visible to the imagination of the listeners.

Actors have to practise many skills, but the first and most important of these is the use of the imagination. The script of any play will remain uninteresting if the reader is not ready to use his mind's eye. No one can ever become an actor unless at the very first reading of a play he is able to look at his colleagues sitting around in ordinary dress in a familiar place and begin to feel that in some other dimension they are coming to life in another place and time – perhaps as sentinels on duty at midnight on the haunted battlements of a castle in Denmark.

It has been argued that it is possible to play Shakespeare's plays without scenery at all, because he always sets the scene and suggests the atmosphere in his choice of words. Do you agree?

1.2   Preparing for the task

The question as to whether this play should be produced in the style, costume and setting of its own day will be discussed in Unit 6 of this chapter, but it is far more important for the actors to get the *style* of movement right than to aim for period accuracy. The overall pattern of movement is one of formality

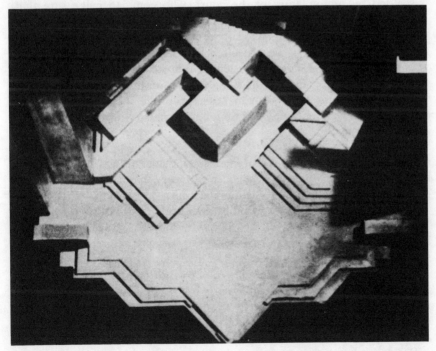

1b   The design for the Broadhurst Theatre production. New York, 1931 by Norma Bel Geddes.

as might be expected in a play set for the most part at the court of an absolute monarch. There is a strict order of precedence in which everyone knows his place and makes appropriate obeisances, courtesies and acknowledgements. So it is necessary for all actors to have an agreed form for such movements. Below this formality, there is a pattern of intrigue and espionage and smiling treachery which will render some of the courtesies somewhat ironical. How does the actor signal what lies behind the politeness of such characters as Osrick and Rosencrantz and Guildenstern?

Intrigue in turn gives way to violence. This pattern of formality, intrigue and violence also affects the relationships and behaviour both within and between the two families in the centre of the play – those of the King and of Polonius. How and when does this occur? In performance, the general framework of formality is maintained by the attendant lords and ladies together with the servants and soldiers.

● To understand this in practice, let the entire company work out and present a processional sequence between the first two scenes of the play. First of all, lower servants under the direction of upper servants, whom they treat with appropriate courtesy, enter carrying various items of furniture required by the King for his council and set them in place. Then come the junior ladies of the court, perhaps a little excited so that they are scolded by senior ladies of the court, who come to make sure that everything is correct for the Queen, who does not enter yet. In the meantime, pages and gentlemen of the court bring in the maps, books and documents of state to be consulted by the King, who also delays his entrance. Then the men-at-arms enter to make sure there is no assassin lurking anywhere. Finally the officer of the day gives the signal for a trumpet to sound. Everybody makes appropriate obeisance to the King as he enters with his family and senior noblemen following in strict order of precedence.

Of course, much of the stiffness of Jacobean movements was imposed by the limitations of the costumes. It could also be argued that the limitations of the costumes reflected the formality of life at court.

The dances of the times demonstrate both formality and violence. Whether it is intended to set the play in period or not, actors will find it helpful and enjoyable to try two contrasting seventeenth-century dances, such as the slow and stately pavane and the vigorous galliarde.

Hamlet, often though of as a play full of words, contains much vigorous action. There is a large number of parts for young and active men. (How many?) Many of these men carry weapons and some actually use them. (Who? In which scenes?) There is a great deal of falling in death, including a death by poison. (For whom?)

Besides general movement practice there is need to work upon stage fights, with and without weapons, and stage falls of different kinds. English actors are famous throughout the world for their skill in swordplay. One reason for this is that there are so many fights in Shakespeare and so many lingering deaths. Stage fights of all kinds depend upon trust between the actors involved. Never try to set a duel or other fight until the actors have worked together long enough to be able to rely upon each other especially at those moments which are most exciting to an audience and most potentially dangerous to the actors. (See Chapter 2.5 for preparatory exercises to be used in preparing a fight.)

One group of actors who should have specially stylised movements are the visiting Players. The first entrance is usually made acrobatic, almost like a circus entry.

● Form groups, to make this into an exciting scene using music if you wish or simply noisy vocalisation. Aim for originality, and bear in mind that each of the players has his own individual personality. Compare this scene with the deliberate parody of it in Tom Stoppard's play *Rosencrantz and Guildenstern are Dead*.

● Try to reproduce the dumbshow from Act Three, Scene 2. The actors must take it seriously; the court may not. There are similar dumbshows in other plays of this period, notably in *The White Devil* by John Webster.

For further notes on movement work see **Unit 2** in other chapters and *Theatre Games* by Clive Barker. For general technical practice see *The Actor and His Body* by Litz Pisk.

In Act Three Scene 2, Hamlet, speaking as a playwright to his actors, gives them some advice. Every actor should not only practise this speech but also be aware if any of the criticisms are likely to apply to him. If he does not know himself, perhaps some of his candid friends will be ready to tell him whether or not he is a 'mouther' or a 'hand-sawyer'. It is hoped that these days no actor struts or bellows, but it is regrettably likely that there will still be exhibitionist comedians, ready to get a cheap laugh at whatever cost.

John Barton, Associate Director to the Royal Shakespeare Company, together with a number of very experienced actors, devoted a television series on Channel 4 to exploring what special difficulties confront the actor playing Shakespeare on the modern stage. He began by pointing out that the modern actor must find out his own synthesis between the modern tradition of writing and acting which is based upon reproducing everyday conversational speech and the older Elizabethan tradition of 'heightened language'. At one time it used to be accepted that Shakespeare's lines had to be spoken in a special kind of voice aiming at the achievement of 'beautiful' effects, but Barton and his actors agreed that it is best for the actor to begin by aiming for *truth*, especially truth of situation and character. The methods of Stanislavsky (see Chapter Three) will apply to Shakespeare as well as to Chekhov.

Consider the following simple exchange:

POLONIUS: What do you read, my lord?
HAMLET: Words, words, words.

The actors will have no way of knowing how to play these lines until they have agreed upon the circumstances surrounding the characters. Here are some possible circumstances. Consider each in turn to see how it affects the way the lines are spoken.

(a) Polonius wishes to know what Hamlet is reading, but Hamlet does not wish to be interrupted.

(b) Polonius thinks that what Hamlet is reading may provide him with a clue about Hamlet's state of mind, but Hamlet blandly brushes him off.

(c) Polonius, genuinely thinking that Hamlet may be truly mad, tries to divert him. Hamlet, realising this, plays up by pretending to be melancholy mad.

● Invent other circumstances arising from different possible relationships between Hamlet and Polonius. Then consider the complete dialogue between them beginning at 'How does my good lord Hamlet?' (Act Two, Scene 2). Before playing it through consider what each man is thinking but does not express in words.

If actors always remain true to character and situation, they will keep the interest of an audience, even when speaking a **soliloquy**. This kind of set speech always presents special problems. If the actor is tempted to use a soliloquy as a chance to display his skill in a solo performance, then he is almost certain to bore the audience. In the television series mentioned earlier, John Barton said this:

What about the most famous soliloquy of all? With 'To be or not to be' there are an infinite number of possibilities, but I think that if we're in doubt there's one very good rule to follow. In acting . . . we must see the complexities, but we must always try to be *simple*. . . . In dialogue a character reaches out to another character and in a soliloquy a character reaches out to the audience. . . . An actor must make the audience listen and follow the story-line of the thoughts. There will be no danger then of people switching off till the dreaded long speech is over.

Refer to the Glossary for a definition of the term **soliloquy** and then try to apply John Barton's advice.

1.3   Exploring the background

There is something in this story of a Renaissance prince which can strike a chord in a modern student, so that he feels sympathy with Hamlet and takes his side against those who oppose him. The emotions expressed by the characters in *Hamlet* are simply our own emotions 'writ large' and carried to extreme. Everybody has experienced within himself, however briefly, the impulse to violence against those he knows and loves. Afterwards, we may laugh and say, 'I could have killed you when . . .', but for that very brief moment the impulse was real. The emotions that we experience in real life differ not in kind, but only in degree, from the emotions displayed in **classic tragedy**. With us the emotions remain under control. With the characters in tragedy, the circumstances are such that this cannot be so. If actors are to attempt to play classic tragic roles, then they must try to understand how the characters feel and why they are driven to act as they do.

It is sometimes useful to improvise situations analogous to those in a play, setting them in present and familiar circumstances. Here are a few such situations. (The characters may be taken by actors of either sex. This is an attempt to correct the predominance of male parts in *Hamlet*, which is unfair to the female student.)

(a)   A young person (A) 'accidentally' encounters two others (B) and (C). All three were friends at school, but A has drifted apart from the other two. B and C now seem somewhat shallow to A, who begins to wonder why they have suddenly become so friendly. A forces the truth out of them. They have been sent by A's parents as spies. What are they trying to find out?

(b)   A widowed parent (A) breaks the news to child (B) that a second marriage is about to take place. A very short time has elapsed since the death of the other parent.

(c)   A is a second husband/wife, trying to make friends with B, child of the first marriage. This does not succeed because of character conflict.

(d)   A young person (A) distrusts an older and important person (B), who is asking him personal questions. A replies without appearing rude, but evades the questions.

(e)   A, the brother of B, believes that B has been in some way betrayed by C, who was B's boyfriend. Set up two confrontations. In one, the boyfriend is innocent, in the other he is not.

This is by no means the only way to use improvisation when studying a play. See Unit 3 throughout the book.

1c   Osrick and Hamlet, The Greenwich Theatre, 1974.

1.4   Characters and relationships

When an actor is given a part in a new play, the first thing he is likely to do is to thumb through the script looking for his own part to see how big it is. Then he settles down to read it more carefully to see what sort of person he is being asked to portray. Consider one of the 'cameo parts' first, such as Osrick, who first appears in Act Five, Scene 2. The part may well have been written for a promising apprentice. What clues has Shakespeare given the actor?

Hamlet calls him a 'water fly' and tells him to put his bonnet to its right use. Here is a fine comic picture for the actor to realise. How do you think he would enter? How does he bow to Hamlet? What exactly does he do with that bonnet which Hamlet finds so amusing or irritating? Play the scene through to bring out the comedy, not only between Hamlet and Osrick but allowing Horatio to join in. But beware of fixing a character too soon. There are more questions to ask about him. Whose side is Osrick on? Is he merely the fool that he seems to be? When he reappears later in the scene, we see that he is the master of ceremonies at the duel. Is he in the plot against Hamlet? Does he know about the poison? In the nineteenth century, Osrick seems to have been played simply as a comic courtier – a young man trying to impress and overdoing it. More recently he has been played as a villain pretending to be an eccentric. So try playing the scene again so that Osrick still seems amusing to Hamlet but makes the audience unwilling to trust him.

However any character is eventually played, the actor must be prepared to justify the interpretation.

● Follow the appearance of any single character through the play, noting all the factual clues that the author has planted. What is his rank or position in society? Is he rich or poor? Is he in a position to influence other people? Note also connections and relationships. With whom has he family connections or professional relationships or ties of friendship? Who are his enemies, rivals or opponents?

It is not until an actor has absorbed all the information given by the author that he is entitled to start inventing details of characterisation.

When actors have tried out their characters by rehearsing one or two scenes, they should be ready to test their knowledge in the game called *Final Interview*.

● Imagine yourself to have been one of the more important characters in the play, but you are now dead. You are therefore in a position to answer Hamlet's famous question about what dreams may come when we have shuffled off this mortal coil. In your dream you face a panel of polite but persistent interrogators. The session may begin like this:

Q: What is your name, please?
A: Polonius.
Q: How did you come to be here?
A: I was killed.
Q: How?
A: I was stabbed through an arras in the Queen's room.
Q: What were you doing there?

1.5 Rehearsing the scene

Having cast the play, most directors go on to a reading. Cuts are agreed and duly noted. Then the play is read right through with as few pauses as possible in order to get the general sense. Some directors like to have several readings. Some like to use improvisation parallel to the early readings. Sooner or later, however, the actors feel the need to get up and move about, book in hand. They are now ready for the *setting rehearsal*.

● Follow this process in detail with one particular scene – Act One, Scene 5, for instance – working in teams of four: director, two actors and stage-manager.

At first sight, the long speeches given to the Ghost look very intimidating to the actor who would have to speak them. In practice they are often reduced in length. Which lines are necessary to the telling of the story? Which lines do not tell the audience any more about the plot, but may develop the character in some way? Which lines do not appear to do either? In the first category are lines such as 'I am thy father's spirit', and 'If ever thou didst thy dear father love . . . Revenge his foul and most unnatural murder.' The Ghost's first speech could be cut down to just these three lines without in any way affecting the plot, but since a play is more than its plot there is a case for restoring lines 10–13 which give a reason for the Ghost to walk at all. (He is being punished.) The rest of the speech, all about the horrors of hell, although famous and possibly thrilling in its time, may not be the greatest of poetry and most directors cut it without any qualms.

● Now work through the rest of the scene up to line 91 to complete the cutting using the criteria suggested. If it is a *plot line* or a *character line*, then keep it in. If it seems to fill neither function, consider what it does for atmosphere and mood.

Atmosphere lines are usually well worth keeping, because of their tremendous power in evoking both physical environment and psychological mood. Shakespeare's finest poetry frequently appears in this sort of line.

There are many ways in which a simple stage direction such as '*Enter* GHOST *and* HAMLET' can be realised. There are the practical problems arising from the ending of the previous scene. Hamlet and the Ghost left the stage (which way?) to be followed later by Horatio and Marcellus, so which way can they re-enter without upsetting credibility? More than that, *how* does the Ghost enter? With what sort of gesture does he beckon Hamlet on? How long is it before Hamlet speaks? Or do we hear him speaking off as we see the Ghost enter?

● Try this entrance several times in different ways to see which way seems to meet the writer's intention. Work through the whole scene, first as a simple walk-through to get moves and relative position right, then let the actors give as much expression to the reading as they can.

If this makes some of the moves come out differently, so much the better if the actors *feel* that it is right. It is the director's job to check that it *looks* right.

The director should, of course, check the work from more than one position in the auditorium.

How does Hamlet speak the soliloquy? (See Unit 2.) The actor should prepare the speech in the light of what has happened to Hamlet up to this point in the play. He no longer has any doubts about the Ghost. He now knows that he has in fact spoken to his own dead father and he believes what the Ghost has told him. Try to speak this speech so that Hamlet *shares* his feelings with the audience.

● Now rearrange the teams to include three actors and continue with the rest of the scene in the same way, cutting, reading, characterising, finding the mood and then trying a walk-through.

After the soliloquy the actor playing Hamlet must give the actors playing Horatio and Marcellus enough emotional atmosphere when they enter. The main difficulty here is to maintain the tension that has been built up. The falconer's cries between Hamlet and Marcellus could be cut but there is a further difficulty. Consider how Hamlet would speak the following lines:

O wonderful! . . .
No, you will reveal it. . . .
But you'll be secret? . . .
There's never a villain dwelling in all Denmark
But he's an arrant knave.

They make very little sense at first reading, but perhaps Shakespeare did not intend them to do so. The more the actor tries to make sense out of them, the less he is likely to succeed unless he has some idea of what is happening inside Hamlet's mind, which is both excited and confused by the Ghost's revelations. Hamlet is thinking and feeling on several levels at once.

There is an excitement, even elation. The Ghost has told him that the suspicions that he held but did not express were true and justified. This makes him say, 'O wonderful!'

There is also the realisation that he has been let into an important and dangerous secret. When Horatio says, 'What news, my Lord?' Hamlet is tempted to tell him straightaway, but he checks himself: 'No, you will reveal it.' Yet he is bursting to tell somebody. He feels the need to tell these men who are perhaps the only people he can trust. But can he? 'But you'll be secret?'

Perhaps he will tell them that he has found out that his uncle is a murderer and adulterer – 'There's never a villain dwelling in all Denmark . . .' – but he stops; even as he says this he doubts whether it is wise to name the King as a villain, so he ends his sentence rather feebly in a sort of lame joke: '. . . But

13

he's an arrant knave.' This baffles Horatio, who says, 'There needs no ghost, my Lord, come from the grave/To tell us this.' What does Horatio think and feel at this point? Does he begin to doubt the sanity of his friend the Prince?

Meanwhile Hamlet is thinking, perhaps, 'I can't tell them, at least not yet. I must get rid of them.' The next six lines are spoken almost at random, like a man in a state of shock. His mind is now filled by the image of his unhappy father, this ghost now suffering in hell. He says, 'I will go pray'. Horatio, still not understanding and becoming worried says, 'These are but wild and whirling words, my lord.' (It is worth noting here that it is more important for the actor to bring out Horatio's *feeling* for his friend than for him to elocute this rather effective line.) Hamlet realises that he has hurt his friend's feelings and apologises. Marcellus is silent, but he has his own feelings.

This method of analysis is very useful and indeed necessary to the preparation of scenes as complex as this. The actor has to convey meaning and feeling on more than one level at the same time. What he conveys to another character on the stage may not be the whole emotional truth. There is another meaning underneath which has to be conveyed to the audience. Note that this is the first time that Hamlet is seen to behave in a manner that could be called mad. The rest of this scene, with the Ghost *'crying from below'*, may seem a little odd to modern audiences, but could be worth attempting, if the setting-problem can be solved.

● Now try working towards a prepared rehearsal of Act Three, Scene 1, using the same methods. It is a key scene. Directors and actors must face and answer some of the important questions in the play, such as 'Is Hamlet really mad?', 'Is Ophelia in the plot against him?'

1.6 Realisation

Nowadays the term 'design' sometimes includes poster, programme and other publicity layouts. There is often a motif, logo or colour pattern running all through the artistic work connected with a particular production. What might it be for *Hamlet*? A sword and a skull, perhaps in black and white?

● Discuss the general policy with regard to the kind of setting best suited to the play. What are the arguments for and against setting *Hamlet* much as it was when it was first presented? Nineteenth-century producers aimed at detailed realism in scenery, costumes and furnishings. What are the advantages and drawbacks of their approach?

However it is decided to set it, the play is very episodic, with frequent changes of place. How are such changes to be indicated? How does the

1d *Hamlet* in 1920s dress.

necessary furniture get into position? If the scene-shifters must work in full sight of the audience, then might it not be better to dress them in costume similar to that worn by the actors? Indeed, could they not become actors – playing as attendant lords and ladies?

The so-called 'historically accurate' costume frequently proves to be difficult to obtain and is often quite useless for its purpose when it arrives. When dressing a character consider what sort of person the actor is trying to create. Without for the moment, trying to design a costume, play the game of *colour, texture and shape*.

● What sort of colours do you associate with Polonius? Is he a faded grey person? Or a plum-coloured person?

● Consider texture. Is he a smooth person or a loosely textured person? In shape, is he rounded? Squarish? Or thin and angular? (This is quite a fascinating game to play with real people in mind.)

● Now return to the question of historical period, which need not be the seventeenth century, of course. Indeed, there are arguments for setting the play farther back in time.

There have been several modern-dress productions in this century. Even if a producer does not intend to use contemporary style in costume, it sometimes helps to understand a character like Hamlet by wondering how he would dress if he were alive today. An obvious solution to this problem might be to dress him as a student – but what sort of student? And how should Ophelia be dressed? There are many questions to answer before we can claim that our costumes are completely designed for every character. Hamlet is usually dressed in black. Where, in the text, does it say so? The ghost is in armour. What sort of armour? Does King Claudius wear a crown at any time during the play? Should the Queen wear mourning at Ophelia's funeral? Who else might do so? Nobody wears the same costume every day in real life, so why should we expect these generally wealthy characters to have no change of garments?

1e   Male actors as Gertrude and Ophelia.

● Plot costume changes for the Queen throughout the play. Try it with other characters. Even Hamlet himself, or does he never change his clothes? If so, why should this be?

Similar procedures can be used for the design of props, including weapons. Ophelia's bouquet of wild flowers must suit with her costume. The Gravediggers' tools must not look too modern and must look as if they have been used a lot. Osrick's sword may appear almost too exquisite, but it must look sharp and deadly to match the man himself.

● Finally, assemble your designs for costumes and props and imagine them being worn or used by the actors who will play the various parts.

This is the acid test. All the designs should seem to belong naturally together, but humanity being what it is you may have to modify to fit some actors. Every actor in an ideal world would fit his costume as easily as he fits his part, but suppose your Hamlet has every attribute for his part except height, or, as in the case of Burbage, slimness?

2
'As You Like It' by William Shakespeare

Probably written about 1599 and published in 1623. The plot is taken from *Rosalynde or Euphues' Golden Legacy* by Thomas Lodge, which may well have been popular reading at the time. Robert Armin, clown, musician, composer and minor playwright, may have played Touchstone. The part of Rosalind, originally played by a young male actor, is longer and more dominant than many female roles in Shakespeare's plays. It has therefore attracted many great actresses. The references are to the Penguin edition, 1968.

2.1. Barriers across the path

A production committee set up to consider this play would be likely not only to meet similar problems to those raised by *Hamlet* (see previous chapter) but to discover even more.

As You Like It is not as long as *Hamlet*, so there is less need for cutting. The plot is very simple. Some people may say that it is too simple. It takes you very little time to arrive at the plot line, but it seems remarkably thin. Characters in the tragedies always have strong motives for their actions. Claudius in *Hamlet* has his ambition and his lust for the Queen to drive him to murder his brother; but just why does Oliver de Boys make his brother's life such a misery? The only reason given is that he is the wicked brother, while Orlando is the good brother, as in a folk tale. Why does this play work in the theatre so well, in spite of the childish simplicity of the plot?

2a The frontispiece for Rowe's edition. (1709).

● To answer this question, make another analysis of the play, working in
   five groups. This time, simply note the number of characters on the stage
   at different times in each act.

Act One, Scene 1, opens with just two characters, then there are three, and
although new characters are always coming and going there are never more
than four characters on set until suddenly the stage becomes crowded for the
wrestling-match. When this is over there are once more three characters left
to carry the story a stage further. This pattern recurs throughout the play,
which ends with a formal and elaborate masque involving all the principal
characters.

● When this analysis is complete, concentrate upon the crowd scenes. What opportunity do they give the producer for songs, dances, movement of all sorts, colourful costumes and spectacle generally? Now look at the small cast scenes. Make a list of the characters who appear in them. Who appears most often? Who dominates most of the scenes? What skills and attributes must the various actors bring to their parts?

It becomes obvious that there is a central role for a star performer, whose gender is less important than having outstanding acting skill. There is a role for a handsome, attractive and physically strong leading man. We shall need a comedian who can sing and preferably be able to dance, and a character-actor with a good voice and a sense of humour. Also, there is a second leading lady who must not only be pretty but know how to time some tricky dialogue. There are several interesting minor comic parts, judicially placed to provide a change of flavour to prevent the main storyline becoming a bore. Some of the characters must not only be actors in the crowd scenes but singers and musicians as well. What *kind* of entertainment in the theatre today would make similar demands on the performers? The obvious parallels are pantomime on the one hand, with its transvestism and its folk-story plot, and the spectacular musical on the other. With this in mind, it can be seen that credibility and consistency of plot are no longer necessary. There seems to be no moral lesson, no underlying philosophy in this play. The only philosopher in the cast is Jaques and he is a charlatan.

Do you agree that *As You Like It* is not so much a title as an advertisement? Is it fair to say the author wrote this play for commercial reasons only? Whether he did or not, do not presume that to produce such an entertainment is in any way easier than producing a grand tragedy. Indeed, in many ways it is harder. Since *what* is being done may seem so very trivial, then *how* it is done becomes of paramount importance. The producer will have to find performers of outstanding talent. He must be able to fill the stage with exciting colour, movement and sound several times, each time different and more exciting up to a really impressive grand finale. Also, it is better not to be too sure that this comedy is trivial. If we concentrate upon theatrical effectiveness and also see a good production of it, we may discover that the play is, as one of its editors has said, 'a complex and subtle vision of reality'.

The author is scarcely helpful at times. Exposition scenes, such as Act One, Scene 1, are never easy to write, but here Shakespeare seems to have taken no trouble at all. How can a producer help the actor who plays Orlando to get and hold the attention of the audience with that long and potentially boring opening speech? Nineteenth-century producers, picking up an idea from a line that says Orlando is in his brother's orchard, gave their designers a chance to make a glorious setting of apple trees all in blossom. Through the trees the handsome and athletic Orlando enters with his faithful servant, perhaps even swinging from bough to bough! This picturesque approach was quite rightly condemned by the critics, but there are just a few arguments in its favour. What are they?

Obviously, Orlando and Adam must be given something to do during this speech. What sort of things?

● Working in pairs as master and servant, Elizabethan or modern, devise some plausible activity to engage them, such as clothing being repaired or weapons sharpened or even some game being played to alleviate boredom.

The *chain of love* is a common plot-device. Chekhov uses it (see Chapter Three) as well as Shakespeare. So do TV script-writers today. But in this play there is an added complication. Not only does Silvius love Phebe, who loves Ganymede, but Ganymede loves no woman because 'he' is Rosalind, who loves Orlando, who is wooing Ganymede, who is pretending to be Rosalind . . .

This leads us to the next question, which is about the nature of sexual impersonation on the stage. What is the difference, between this Shakespearean impersonation and 'drag'? Or the transvestism of English pantomime?

These are fascinating topics to discuss, but there is another, more directly relevant. For three hundred years the great female roles in Shakespeare's plays have been played by women and it has been taken for granted that this should be so. Most people would say that an actress of quality would surely give a better performance of Rosalind than any of Shakespeare's treble-voiced boy apprentices. This may very well be true, but it presumes that the major leading female parts were written for boys. In fact, they may well have been written for young adult male actors of some considerable experience and talent. The performances given by these actors might very well have been more comparable with that of the best actresses today. The National Theatre presented an all-male production of *As You Like It* in 1967 with Ronald Pickup as Rosalind. With the success of this production there was some discussion as to whether male actors were in fact better vocally equipped to play Shakespearean heroines. Some critics argue that, because women's rib-cages are smaller than men's, women could not take in and hold enough breath to sustain the very long phrases which are needed at high moments in Elizabethan drama.

Here is a piece to test this theory. It comes towards the end of the play in Act Five, Scene 2, and is spoken to Orlando by Rosalind while still disguised as Ganymede.

Nay, 'tis true. There was never anything so sudden but the fight of two rams, and Caesar's thrasonical brag of 'I came, saw, and overcame.' For your brother and my sister no sooner met but they look'd; no sooner look'd but they lov'd; no sooner lov'd but they sigh'd; no sooner sigh'd but they ask'd one another the reason; no sooner knew the reason but they sought the remedy; and in these degrees have they made a pair of stairs to marriage, which they will climb incontinent, or else be incontinent before marriage. They are in the very wrath of love, and they will together. Clubs cannot part them.

What is the minimum number of pauses for breath needed to make this speech sound most effective? At first, an actor may be tempted to keep the phrases short or at least to rest at every full stop and semi-colon, but this would defeat the intention of the passage which is to convey a picture of two people somewhat ridiculously falling in love at first sight and rushing into each others arms with remarkable speed.

No actor, female or male, can achieve the intended effect without careful phrasing and plenty of practice.

● Begin by saying the word 'thrasonical' several times at increasing speed until it trips naturally off the tongue.

● Then try speaking the whole phrase, 'There was never anything so sudden but the fight of two rams, and Caesar's thrasonical brag of "I came, saw, and overcame." '

● Finally, practise the whole speech until you can convey the meaning and the sense of fun with absolutely minimum pauses.

One further barrier needs to be considered. It arises from confusions about the various shades of meaning given to the word **comedy**. We can probably agree without too much debate that this play is intended to make the audience smile more often than it makes it laugh, but sometimes it does not seem to be very clear exactly where the point of the joke may lie for a contemporary audience. Not only has the language changed over four hundred years (see Chapter 1.1) but many jokes excellent in their time have become pointless. Here is an extract from *Zigger Zagger* by Peter Terson:

ZIGGER [*as narrator*]: Harry has a sister. Nice girl. Nice house. A Do-It-Yourself house. All paint and glitter, made with pre-packed nails, cut-to-size hardboard and contemporary pre-packed coat-hangers with nobs on in blues and reds. A doorbell like ice-cream chimes plays the first bar of 'Greensleeves'. A land-locked little paradise with plastic palm trees and a muralette of Tahiti on the wall. She's even got a Do-It-Yourself Husband. Made him out of an anatomy kit. Seriously though, nice girl. She's had her dreams, of course. Once fell in love with a disc jockey . . . .

Is this still as funny as it was when first produced in 1967? Does it already show signs of dating? What footnotes might scholars have to compile if the play became an English classic and was still being studied in 2367?

Now try the following, which is extracted from no play ever written. It is a piece of synthetic Elizabethan dialogue written for two clowns of either sex. It is not intended to be complete nonsense but to suggest more sense than it actually possesses.

> CLOWN A: Greetings goodman fishwife or goodwife fishman, whatso'er you be.
>
> CLOWN B: Get thee gone thou knock-kneed ninny.
>
> CLOWN A: Nay, an thou call me knock-kneed I'll need to knock thy knees sirrah.
>
> CLOWN B: Away before I knock thy knees down to their uncles.
>
> CLOWN A: Uncles quotha? Ankles, mean'st thou?
>
> CLOWN B: Nay! Uncles! For since thy knees be kissing cousins it is to their uncles they will fly when knocked down.
>
> *They fight.*

● Rehearse the scene privately in pairs using the dialogue to explore the possibilities for comic action. When you are ready, try it upon your colleagues. Then discuss the various devices by which you can use a script to make people laugh.

If you were completely unsuccessful do not despair. The gift of comedy is not given to everyone, but a good comedian can make his audience laugh with a very old joke or, indeed, no joke at all. Touchstone is not the only source of humour in the play. Rosalind and Celia are both witty, and Jaques though not himself a humorist is frequently a cause of laughter in others. It is a mistake to regard Touchstone as the clown and expect him to make the audience go into roars of laughter at his every appearance. It is better to treat him simply as a character like all the others. It is true that he is a professional entertainer, but his jokes need not always come off. He also exists in other relationships. He is companion to Rosalind and Celia, would-be seducer of Audrey and has other roles to fulfil. What are they?

2.2 Preparing for the task

No Shakespeare play can be prepared without paying attention to the spoken word, especially to the verse. Hamlet's advice to the players should be engraved on the memory of all actors (see Chapter 1.2). Every actor should also practise Jaques' famous speech 'All the world's a stage . . .' (Act Two, Scene 7). This was written as a set-speech for a good actor.

● Speak the speech aloud, book in hand. It is easy to visualise the various characters as Jaques calls them to life. Put the book down and become one of them, in mime, or in a short scene with dialogue. For instance, when the schoolboy reaches school at last, is the master awaiting him? When the lover has written his ballad and given it to his lady, is she annoyed, impressed or amused? How does he deliver it to her?

Such an exercise could lead us into research. For instance, what might be in the satchel carried by the whining schoolboy? What does the lover use in writing his woeful ballad? What weapons does the soldier carry?

The speech could be made the basis of a 'Masque of Seven Ages', not necessarily restricted to a seventeenth-century setting.

2.3 Exploring the background

Refer to Chapter 6.3 for details of the game of *Nobs and Peasants*. Once you have played it you will have been reminded of the naked political facts of a period which nevertheless gave the world many elegant works of art, including this particular play. But, since this is a gentle comedy, we must

2b The mock marriage scene.

soften the Brechtian harshness of our approach by introducing some elements of dignity and grace. By far the best way to do this is by practising and using the dances of the period.

If you are fortunate enough to be able to work with a choreographer you will have no difficulty in finding dances suitable for each of the little 'masques' which occur throughout the play. There are two basic movement patterns within the comedy. One, associated with the court, is dignified showing its skill in matters of courtesy and romance. The other is jolly, earthy with the skills of the herdsman.

● Practise these in pairs, aiming for contrast. If you have no choreographer, you can still at least make an approach to dancelike movements by listening to recordings of the music of the period and improvising either courtly or rustic movements to them.

The Jacobeans did not hit people on the head, as in the game of *Nobs and Peasants*. If a peasant offended, he could be hanged. If a nobleman offended his sovereign, he could be beheaded. To look at the costumes of the period is to be reminded of this frightening fact by the way that the ruff separates the head from the body.

● Imagine that you are wearing Jacobean costume. Think where it will restrict your movements if you are a noble person and especially if you are a noble lady. Then think how you would feel a sense of freedom if you were a nobleman who could dress like a peasant or a noble woman who could dress as a man!

The basic structural joke of the play is the *chain of love*.

● In groups, work out such a chain (or perhaps a *ronde*) in which A declares his love to B, who rejects him. B then approaches C and is rejected. C goes to D and so on. To make it an interesting technical challenge, make a rule that no one in the group uses exactly the same words or gestures as anyone else, either in declaring love or rejecting it.

● Use mime, or very simple dialogue. At first you need not follow the plot line of the play, but once you have practised a little try to capture the *essence* of it.

● Introduce the element of disguise by using simple masks-on-sticks. (How many must Rosalind have?)

● Use the ideas that you have already evolved for a courtly dance and so turn your 'chain of love' into a dignified but none the less entertaining performance.

25

RENNER LEARNING RESOURCE CENTER
ELGIN COMMUNITY COLLEGE
ELGIN, ILLINOIS 60123

2.4 Characters and relationships

How far is it possible to say that any of the characters in this play are real? Of course, it can be said that no character in any play is real. Before we get too involved in basic philosophical questions, perhaps we can agree that there are degrees of reality. Every character in a play or novel is an invention by a writer, but some characters are based upon direct observation of life while other characters are derived from previous works of fiction. How far is this true of *As You Like It*? Which characters seem to be derived and which observed?

● Try putting them into contemporary dress and surroundings.

● Imagine Rosalind as a student with Jacques as her tutor. Consider how they might be dressed and how his study might be furnished. Set up a confrontation between them.

● When you perform, do not bother to set the scene with more than token furniture and do not waste time obtaining the correct costume. Describe it instead. For instance:

> Good afternoon. I am Dr Jaques and I am awaiting the arrival of my student Rosalind. Charming girl, but spends too much time wandering in the woods. I am in my study which is littered and piled high with all my philosophical writings which nobody ever publishes and I am wearing my usual mixture of three old three-piece suits which I have been wearing for the last thirty years . . . .

Audiences will be entitled, when you have finished, to challenge the actors' reasons for what they have said and done in the scene and it must be justified by reference to the text of the play.

● Working in groups of two or three, arrange similar meetings for Touchstone, Orlando, Charles the wrestler or one of the shepherds or shepherdesses in the play.

(To take the character study deeper, refer to Chapter 1.4 and prepare to play the game of *Final Interview*.)

Of Rosalind it has been said that she is everybody's (or is it every man's?) ideal woman. Do you agree?

2.5 Rehearsals

The first ensemble scene is centred round the wrestling-match, but it would be a mistake to begin with the match itself. It is far better to regard the match

RENNER LEARNING RESOURCE CENTER
ELGIN COMMUNITY COLLEGE
ELGIN, ILLINOIS 60123

2c The wrestling match.

as the highest point of a pyramid and to begin by laying a foundation of trust based upon shared experience. While only two actors actually wrestle with each other, it is good for the entire company to acquire the skill of stage combat, for the sake of what they may learn incidentally. To prepare for this, use a series of *trust* exercises.

● In pairs, experiment with communication without speech between two partners – one 'blind', one sighted. The sighted one leads his partner round, over and through obstacles using minimum tactual signals.

● Another method is for one partner to lie relaxed upon the floor. He is then rearranged as far as the disposition of his limbs will allow. The arranging partner then has to take his place in an identical attitude and be himself rearranged, and so on.

A basic combination of handling and trust skills is sometimes called *Drunken Sailor* and sometimes *Trust Circle*.

● One person with eyes closed stands in the middle of a circle of about six people. He remains upright but can be pushed over so that he falls on to the hands of people behind him who push him away so that he is constantly being moved across and round the circle.

A technical exercise with direct application to stage combat is to work in pairs on assisted falls.

● Having worked out a few stage falls by yourself, get your partner to support your fall. The next step is for him to make it seem as if he is attacking you and forcing you down, when he is actually taking your weight and allowing you to slip safely towards the floor.

● Next, develop a stage fight. Each contestant has supporters behind him, suggesting nasty things to do to his opponent.

This is the raw material for the first ensemble scene in Act One, Scene 2. Rosalind, Celia, Touchstone, and Le Beau are already on the stage, when the Duke enters and the wrestling is about to begin.

For the present, this is merely an experiment in the process of going from a small group scene to a large ensemble scene. So there is no need to bother with the words. Concentrate upon plotting the action.

● Decide what shape and size of area the action will fill.

● Make sure that the people already on the stage have taken up a position as a group that will not impede the entrance of the Duke and his followers.

● Decide *how* the entry should be made. Who enters first? The Duke himself? Some attendants? A lord or two? Do Orlando and Charles enter together or are they in two separate groups with their partisans? Has Charles more supporters than Orlando? Has Orlando any supporters at all?

● Work through the movements in the scene as suggested by the text from the entrance of the Duke to his exit.

If you divide the stage into two areas, one generally downstage occupied by Rosalind and her party and the rest mainly centre and upstage occupied by the Duke and the wrestlers, you will see that the story-line action moves out of the Duke's area into Rosalind's when Orlando is fetched to meet her and the centre of action returns to the middle of the stage just before the wrestling begins.

It is obvious that the lords and attendants must not just stand around staring at the ladies or, worse still, doing nothing at all.

● Invent meaningful activities for as many lords and attendants as are likely to be available. (They should be capable of inventing for themselves.) What is going to be happening while the Duke and Rosalind are speaking together? What is going to be happening during the long series of speeches beginning with Celia's 'Young gentlemen . . .' and continuing to the end of Orlando's long speech? This is about twenty lines. This is where the stage picture can be built up and the actors playing the lords and attendants can begin to apply what they have invented during the earlier games and improvisations.

It may also be necessary to hold back the dialogue in order that action may take precedence. For instance, when the wrestling match is about to begin, should there not be a sudden hushed silence? How is this arranged for? The author is not at all helpful. He gives the most curt stage directions for what can be a fairly lengthy and spectacular piece of action. How long, in fact should they wrestle before Charles is thrown? Finally, in what order do the Duke and his attendants leave the stage? Notice that a new and important relationship has sprung up as the result of the match. Le Beau and Touchstone have left the stage and been replaced by Orlando.

- Be prepared to spend some time on this first ensemble scene; the experience may be useful later. At first consider the lines simply as cues for action. Aim at getting a balance between precise speaking of the text by the principal actors, and the exciting movement of the rest of the cast.

Act Four, Scene 2 is one of the scenes that remind us that the whole play is an artificial entertainment. The playwright has neatly established that Rosalind has to wait two hours for Orlando to return from attending on the Duke. We discover later that he spent some of this time rescuing his wicked brother from a lion, but we never see this scene. (Why not?) Instead, there is an interlude filled by Jaques and the lords, including the song about the killing of the deer. If we consider the play as an entertainment, then this short scene (only fifteen lines long), since it is there only to cover a gap in the plot, must be used as a full-scale 'production number'. It needs imaginative development and is worth experimenting upon.

- Divide into groups. Agree to share performances after a limited time. Use simple costume, lighting, props and, of course, music and dance.

One starting-point is to treat the scene as a sort of ritual. It can be comic, serious or just splendidly picturesque. Perhaps Jaques could be the master of ceremonies and the man who killed the deer be initiated into a secret society of foresters with appropriate honours. This could be slightly sinister, perhaps using shadows effectively, or, remembering the old joke about cuckoldry, it could be very broadly funny.

Later, one of the most difficult scenes in the play occurs. The first half of Act Four, Scene 3, runs in a style to which the audience have become accustomed. Rosalind has been in complete charge of the situation and is

2d Touchstone and Corin.

happily expecting the return of Orlando. She sends Silvius on his way with the sensible advice to be a little less of a sheepish shepherd. '. . . hence, and not a word, for here comes more company'. But instead of the expected Orlando she sees Oliver.

The first question to answer concerns Oliver's appearance. Should he be immediately recognisable to the audience who have not seen him since Act One? He describes himself as a 'wretched ragged man o'ergrown with hair'. Rosalind and Celia do not recognise him, but does he recognise them? The actor playing Oliver has a very difficult part. He has two long narrative speeches, but he must also play a subtle supporting role. In this scene, Rosalind experiences the 'moment of truth' when she faints at hearing of Orlando's danger. The game of pretence is ending and the play is obviously nearly over. Although Rosalind faints because she is seriously in love, this scene must also be a high point in the comedy.

● In groups of four (three actors and a director) try the scene through. Share your performances and be prepared to justify every action.

2.6 Realisation

There are at least two opposing views about the best way to stage this play. One group argues that since the play is set for the most part in a forest, then it is an ideal choice of play for production in the open air and by daylight. Others say that, since the forest is not in any way real, and no more than a literary convention, the play can only be performed successfully in a theatre with obviously theatrical costumes and scenery. Which party would you side with? Or have you another, totally different point of view?

We need to be cautious about the meaning of the word *forest*. It does not necessarily imply a deep dark wood. In this forest there are shepherds and sheep as well as lionesses and snakes, and deer. So the forest is much more an otherplace existing once upon a time than a real stretch of land with trees. One interesting compromise might be to consider the problems that might arise if a company tried to set the performance at a nearby stately home, using the grounds as well. Why not go a step farther in combining modern technique with an evocation of the past by setting it as for television or film? In this way it would be possible to use a real orchard for the beginning, a courtyard for the wrestling-match and different parkland venues for the rest of the play.

● Before setting out to fix the locations, having given prior notice and obtained permission from the owners of course, have a meeting to discuss the requirements of each scene.

There is no reason to stick to the entrances and exits as they appear in the text. It adds something to the flavour of the play to have characters 'discovered' by the camera rather than just walking into view through a gap in the hedge. At first sight, it may seem that costume design should be of the seventeenth century, but it may be better to adjust the period so that the costumes go with the main architectural features of the chosen venue. Refer to Unit 6 throughout for further hints.

2e An open-air production in 1884.

31

Whatever period or style chosen for the costumes, there are a number of basic problems to solve. How is the audience to distinguish between courtier and countryman? How will the individual characters, such as Touchstone, Jaques, Charles the wrestler, and Le Beau, be dressed? Each of these has something about him that must be proclaimed in his costume and yet must not contradict the general style of the whole visual effect.

Finally, you may like to know that there was an open-air production of *As You Like It* in 1884, with costumes by Lazenby Liberty. Rosalind as Ganymede wore russet and cinnamon, Touchstone canary and red, and Orlando was played by a lady in dark green plush. Would you use these colours?

3
'The Seagull' by Anton Chekhov

The play was first produced at the Alexandrinsky Theatre, St Petersburg, in 1896. It was an immediate failure. The Moscow Art Theatre's production two years later was a resounding success, so much so that the seagull motif became the badge of the company, appearing on their curtain, posters and programmes.

The play marks a watershed in theatre history. Its first failure may in part be explained by the fact that the Alexandrinsky actors, used to working in what was becoming an old-fashioned style, completely failed to understand it. Equally, its success owed much to Stanislavsky, the director of the Moscow Art Theatre, who saw its potential. Much of Stanislavsky's now famous *Method* was derived from his work on Chekhov's plays.

References are to *The Oxford Chekhov*, vol. 2, translated by R. Hingley (Oxford University Press, 1967).

3.1 Barriers across the path

Chekhov is by far the most popular Russian playwright in Britain. Most British audiences know no other. Although few people these days find the works difficult to understand in performance, many find them very difficult to read. The names of the characters are not only unfamiliar but seem full of consonant-clumps designed to trip an English tongue. The conventions governing the use of personal names are difficult to understand. Characters seem to have several totally different names according to who is addressing them.

Most modern translations include an appendix giving simple rules for pronunciation of Russian names. The reader soon discovers that this is simply a matter of rhythm and stress and with a little practice the difficulties disappear.

Some of the older editions used to set out Russian names in the full order of Christian name, patronymic and family name. For instance, Anton Pavlovich Chekhov had a baptismal name of Anton, and a family name of Chekhov. The middle name simply indicates that this particular Anton was the son of Paul, or Pavel, Chekhov. It is as if in English we had the practice of naming a person John Johnson Jones who in Russian would be Ivan Ivanovich Ivanov. For women, the suffix -*ovna* replaces the male suffix -*ovich*. So a woman whose father was Peter Tolstoy would be, for instance, Olga Petrovna Tolstoy. The use of 'Ivan', 'Ivan Ivanovich' or the pet-name 'Vanya' for the same person would depend upon how well the speaker knew him and the differences in social position between them. Children and servants were usually addressed by the first name only. Once these simple rules are understood, Russian plays become easier to read, but it becomes important when we are studying a Russian play to be aware of the relationships both familial and social between the characters. After all, in England, a lady known formally as Mrs Jones could be called 'Lizzie' by her father, 'Betty' by her mother, 'Mum' by her younger children, 'Elizabeth' by her older children and 'Libby' by her husband, so why should we object when Constantin Treplev is called Kostya by his mother and addressed in other ways by other characters?

There is a further complication peculiar to *The Seagull*. The household in which the action takes place is not a very conventional one. In fact, we discover that it is regarded by Nina's parents as being bohemian. We might expect Constantin's mother to be known as Irina Treplev, but since she is an actress she uses her professional name of Arkadin and in any case is living with the novelist Boris Trigorin. However, only the most recent translators have been helpful enough to point out that she is legally Mrs Treplev.

Why not anglicise altogether? Another Russian classic, Gogol's *The Government Inspector*, was presented on television by the BBC in a version which was set in Wales. The characters were given typically Welsh names. The comedy did not seem to be blunted by this and certainly the play was more immediately understandable. So why not set *The Seagull* in a country house in the Lake District, keeping the professions and relationships of the principal characters? Would it be possible to bring the whole play forward in time to the present?

Not only has Chekhov influenced the writing of British playwrights over the years, but in the same time British actors have been very much affected by the methods of Stanislavsky, who was Chekhov's first successful producer. But the performance at the Alexandrinsky Theatre must have presented problems to both actors and audience. The very first exchange of dialogue bristles with difficulties for them.

The Seagull *by Anton Chekhov*

MEDVEDENKO: Why do you always wear black?
MASHA: I am in mourning for my life, I am unhappy.

They may well have been tempted to classify this dialogue as **romantic tragedy** and therefore have enunciated the lines with a gloomy resonant soulfulness that scarcely bears thinking about. In order to drive away this false notion once and for all, you may try it in that style just once!

But how are we to classify *The Seagull*? Chekhov himself called it a comedy but it cannot be said to end happily. Neither do these opening lines seem to invite the audience to relax and be ready to laugh. None of the characters can be easily typecast. In fact, this play, like Chekhov's other major plays, would have been impossible for the Alexandrinsky actors to perform in any style they knew. How should the actors playing Medvedenko and Masha speak these lines and the eight following speeches? They cannot possibly know this until they have asked and answered some other questions, such as, 'What does each actor need to know about his own character?'

The answer is simple and terrifying. In order to speak the first line in a major play by Chekhov, an actor will need to know *everything* that Chekhov has told him about his character.

This is because Chekhov's characters seem to exist before the curtain goes up. They do not make entrances: they just happen to come into the view of an audience. They go on existing during the time the curtain is down. What is

3a   Chekhov and actors of the Moscow Art Theatre at a rehearsal, 1898.

no more than an interval of a quarter of an hour in front of that curtain may be many years behind it. Or no time at all. The characters will continue to exist during this time and some of them will go on existing after the curtain has fallen for the last time.

In Chekhov's day it was the custom for the author to read the whole play through to the company of actors who were going to play it. Stanislavsky would then have expected the actors to read right through several times more. When actors do this they become aware of certain facts about Medvedenko and Masha which serve as clues to the manner in which the opening lines should be played. Some of these clues are planted in the first eight lines of the play. What do they tell us about the two characters?

● Make your own lists before reading on.

3b   Arkadina and Masha.

The Seagull *by Anton Chekhov*

The Moscow Art actors would have formed the habit of noting and memorising the salient facts about their characters *before* they attempted to learn the lines. So Masha would be aware that Medvedenko is in love with her, but that she is not in love with him. Medvedenko knows that he wants to marry Masha but he is unhappy because he is very badly paid. There are other facts about them not all of which are known to the audience as yet. There is enough material here for a play in itself, but, for Chekhov, these are merely two 'minor' characters in this play.

● Form partnerships, one as Masha and one as Medvedenko. Separate immediately and go apart for a short while to get into character and mood. The time is just *before* the action of the play starts from the point of view of an audience. Think of yourself as being not in the wings of a theatre waiting for a cue to enter on to the stage but as a real person on this particular summer evening in Arkadin's garden wandering about by yourself waiting for Treplev to tell you that he is ready. Masha might be trying to avoid Medvedenko, but Medvedenko is looking for her. He is certain to discover her and as they walk through the gardens they will have a conversation which will lead them naturally into the first lines that Chekhov writes for them:

> Why do you always wear black?
> I am in mourning for my life. I am unhappy.

Chekhov's wife was an actress. He once gave her the following advice about tragic roles: 'Don't look sad . . . people who have been unhappy for a long time and grown used to it are often wrapped up in their own thoughts.'

3.2 Preparing for the task

In the book *An Actor Prepares* there is a story about 'carving the turkey'. One of the Moscow Art Theatre students goes to dinner with an old actor who illustrates some of Stanislavsky's wisdom by pointing out that you cannot eat a whole turkey at once. It must be cut into manageable portions. These portions were known to the students as *units*. So let us now carve up *The Seagull* into units. Chekhov divided the play into acts but those are still too large and complex, so we need much smaller units.

● As you study each act, go through it to decide where one unit ends and another begins. Entrances and exits provide fairly obvious signposts.

In fact, the continental way of writing a play is to give a new scene number whenever a character enters or exits and it is possible that Chekhov followed this practice. Sometimes a unit ends at a moment of crisis, as when, in Act One, Treplev interrupts the performance of his play.

To identify your units you can label them by the names of the characters present. The first unit of the play is therefore 'Masha and Medvedenko'. A larger and more complex unit could have a title of its own such as 'The Play', in Act One, or 'The Game of Lotto', in Act Three. Having done this, you will have a useful outline of the plot for reference.

Stanislavsky was scathing about actors who did not take the trouble to try to perfect their own technique or even to rehearse thoroughly. He was particularly harsh on people who exploited the theatre for personal ends. For instance, he criticised a girl student who had become too aware of her own attractiveness, pointing out that Shakespeare did not write *The Taming of the Shrew* in order that she could use the part of Katharine to show herself off and flirt with her audience from the stage. 'Therefore you must make up your mind, once and for all, did you come here to serve art or to exploit your own personal ends?'

He warned all students that 'clichés will fill out every part in a role which is not already solid with living feeling'. He gave examples of the kind of clichés that could be seen in his own day, such as rubbing the brow with the back of the hand in moments of tragedy. This is still seen on the stage today, yet strangely enough it may well have been invented by the Moscow Art Theatre actress who created the role of Nina in *The Seagull*. It seems to have been so effective that it was immediately imitated, and so became a cliché. Other examples included the use of special voices, such as the 'theatrical tremolo' for high emotion, and covering the eyes and the face with the hands, at the same time mechanically heaving the shoulders, to get the effect of weeping.

This style has been frozen for ever in some of the old silent movies that have survived, but it would be a mistake to think that the use of cliché is dead. Indeed, film has given actors the chance to use more vocal clichés. There is the clipped speech used by actors to portray British officers with literally stiff upper lips, or the throaty breathiness indicating yearning passion; there is the 'mummerset accent' used to portray countrymen and worst of all is the 'funny voice' used by comic actors to cover weak characterisations. Look out for examples of these, have fun in imitating them, but never use them. Bad habits are easily formed and hard to break. Good habits are only acquired in patience and humility. Stanislavsky would tell his students that an actor is like a baby. He must learn to walk and to talk, to look and to see, to listen and to hear.

While we think of him as being mainly concerned with the psychology of the actor we must never forget that there was a very large amount of physical work in the training of his actors. In order for this to be effective the first thing a student had to do was to learn to relax, so that he could use his body economically with a minimum of tension. Students were instructed to study the behaviour of cats. When a cat is about to spring he tenses *only* those muscles he needs for the spring and always relaxes muscles not in use.

● Test your own degree of physical tension by lying on your back on the floor and check whether your entire body from the back of your head to your heels is in contact with the floor. Many people find at first that they are making contact at three or four points only.

Relaxation is a skill that the actor needs to practise. Strangely enough, this is at first tiring, because relaxation is not the same as rest. It is a mistake to imagine that, if you have to play the part of a person under stress, you yourself must become tense. In fact, the converse is true. The more your part calls for the *appearance* of excitement or tension, the more you (the actor) must be relaxed and calm. A relaxed actor will not be 'in the way' of his subconscious mind, which Stanislavsky believed to be the source of all creative energy. For the actor, this energy can only express itself through the actor's voice and body.

Technical work should never be done merely for its own sake, but in order to make the voice and body effective instruments at the disposal of the mind. Every good actor works *intuitively*, but this intuition may be frustrated by sheer lack of physical skill. The act of relaxation makes concentration more easy and permits the subconscious mind to come into play, so that body and mind work together as one. For technical exercises to be carried out regularly, refer to the works of Litz Pisk, Cecily Berry and Clive Barker (see Booklist).

Russian actors are trained to speak on the stage by declaiming the verse of their own great poets in the same way that all British actors must some time or other have practised some of Shakespeare's great speeches (see Chapters One and Two). This gives the actors a respect and a feeling not only for great poetry but for their own spoken language and an awareness of its possibilities.

Here is a brief extract from an earlier play by Chekhov, a comedy called *The Bear*. It has no great psychological depth but is very entertaining. The male character, Smirnov, is extremely angry with Mrs Popov, a pretty young widow who owes him money but refuses to discuss the matter.

SMIRNOV: . . . I don't know how to treat a lady, don't I? Madam, I've seen more women in my time than you have house-sparrows. . . . There have been twenty-one women in my life. Twelve times it was me broke it off, the other nine got in first. Oh yes! Time was I made an ass of myself, slobbered, mooned around, bowed and scraped and practically crawled on my belly. I loved, I suffered, I sighed at the moon, I languished, I melted, I grew cold. I loved passionately, madly, in every conceivable fashion. . . . But now – no thank you very much! I can't be fooled anymore, I've had enough. . . . You must know what women are like, seeing you've the rotten luck to be one. Tell me frankly, did you ever see a sincere, faithful, true woman? You know you didn't. Only the old and ugly ones are true and faithful. You'll never find a constant woman, not in a month of Sundays you won't, not once in a blue moon!

MRS POPOV: Well, I like that! Then who is true and faithful in love to your way of thinking? Not men by any chance?

SMIRNOV: Yes, madam. Men

MRS POPOV: Men! [*Gives a bitter laugh.*] Men true and faithful in love! That's rich, I must say. [*Vehemently*] What right have you to talk like that? Men true and faithful? If it comes to that, the best man I've ever known was my late husband. . . . I loved him passionately, with all my heart as only an intelligent young woman can . . . he carried on with other girls before my very eyes, he was unfaithful to me. . . . But I loved him all the same, and I've been faithful to him. What's more, I'm still faithful and true now that he's dead. I've buried myself alive inside these four walls and I shall go round in these widow's weeds till my dying day.

SMIRNOV: [*with a contemptuous laugh*]. . . . Mysterious and romantic, isn't it? Some army cadet or hack poet may pass by your garden, look up at your windows and think: 'There dwells Tamara, the mysterious princess, the one who buried herself alive from love of her husband.' Who do you think you're fooling?

MRS POPOV: [*flaring up*]. What! You dare to take that line with me!

SMIRNOV: Buries herself alive – but doesn't forget to powder her nose!'

(*Chekhov: Short Plays*, translated by R. Hingley, Oxford University Press, 1969)

● Form groups of three, two actors and a director to give an enjoyable prepared reading.

3.3 Exploring the background

Improvisation in the sense of 'making it up as we go along' existed in the theatre long before Stanislavsky began his work. In true improvisation there is a spontaneity, freshness and sincerity sometimes lacking in professional theatre that has become set in its ways.

Stanislavsky used improvisation both in the training of his actors and in preparing them for specific productions. The object is to encourage creativity in the actors. In his own terminology, the 'magic IF' is used as a lever to get us out of our ordinary surroundings into new and relevant 'given circumstances'. But there must be limits to prevent the exercise from degenerating into self-indulgent daydreaming. Stanislavsky warned his students against a tendency to slip into melodrama. He preferred them to imagine from a basis of probability. He expected them to use their own experiences, memories, reading and study. When studying a specific play, they were expected to research the play for period and place and to pick up any clues provided by the author about their characters.

In the chapter on imagination in *An Actor Prepares* Stanislavsky shows the students sketches for settings for a play about the frozen north:

'Who would believe', said the Director, 'that this was painted by a man who, in all his life, never stirred beyond the suburbs of Moscow? He made an arctic scene out of what he saw around him at home in winter, from stories and scientific publications, from photographs. Out of all that material his imagination painted a picture.'

Over the years many teachers have built upon the original methods and modified them considerably, but nobody has improved upon the concept of the 'magic IF' working within the given circumstances. Here is an exercise along these lines, which is intended to develop creativity. Ideally, this should begin in a fairly quiet atmosphere, perhaps following a period of vigorous activity.

● Sit on the floor and imagine that you are alone. (It does not matter if in fact you are surrounded by your colleagues. As an actor it is your job to share intimate thoughts with hundreds of total strangers, so you must acquire the skill of remaining 'private in public'.)

● Imagine that near you is a door or a gate or a gap in a hedge or a hole in the wall or some other means of passing from where you are to somewhere else. Before you get up to go through the door, gate, gap, hole, or whatever, ask yourself the following questions: Am I inside or outside? Do I <u>want</u> to go or have I <u>got</u> to go through this door, gate, etc.?

● Get up and examine your entrance/exit. Do not be in a hurry. Ask yourself what it looks like. If it is a door, is it a large oak-panelled door studded with nails or a flimsy sort of thing? If it is a gate is it five-barred and made of wood or the sort of wicket gate you have to squeeze through? Can you see beyond it, through it, over it, round it? <u>What</u> do you see? Whatever it is, you can open it or in some way get through. You are now into 'somewhere else'. (Congratulations. You have now made an <u>entrance</u>. So just carry on.)

● Take a few steps forward into the 'somewhere else'. (You are making a <u>journey</u>.) As you go on your journey you may find something interesting. (In which case you have made a <u>discovery</u>.) Or you might meet somebody or some thing. (In which case you will have had an <u>encounter</u>.)

If your imagination is now working pretty strongly so that you feel that you must continue with the story, you are free to do so until you reach a conclusion or you run out of ideas. You may then break out of your privacy and share your story with one of your colleagues. You will notice that the formula we have used – entrance, journey, discovery or encounter – is no more than the basic plotline for many different stories from *Peter Rabbit* to *Hamlet*.

For the sake of tidiness and a feeling of completion you could carry the stories a stage farther and follow the discovery or encounter with perhaps a conflict followed by a resolution and thence to a conclusion.

The plot of any play will tend to follow this pattern and frequently repeat it in miniature in smaller sequences or units of action. In the exercise, you probably chose to be yourself in various 'given circumstances'. You could now repeat the exercise as a character of your own invention or from a play you may be studying.

3.4 Characters and relationships

See Chapter 1.3 for examples of the use of improvisation to explore characters and relationships within a classic play. Then set up improvisations on themes from *The Seagull* using contemporary settings.

How, for instances, might an actress who is highly successful and popular in establishment entertainment react to the news that her son is appearing in the kind of show of which she most strongly disapproves?

What is a contemporary situation parallel to that of Nina and Trigorin? In what other ways could it have been worked out?

What changes would have to be made in plot or character to turn *The Seagull* into a television serial? Justify any adaptation you might make. Consider how you would cast it.

● Go back into the period in which the play is set and as an epilogue to each act prepare and perform a scene based on what the servants think of what has been going on. (Downstairs always knows more than upstairs thinks!)

3.5 Rehearsing the scene

Study the following extract from Act One:

Enter SORIN *and* TREPLEV, *right.*
SORIN: [*leaning on a stick*] Country life doesn't really suit me, boy, and I shall never get used to this place, you can see for yourself. I went to bed at ten o'clock last night and woke at nine this morning, feeling as if all that sleep had glued my brain to my skull or something. [*Laughs.*] Then

I happened to drop off again this afternoon, and now I feel more dead than alive. It's a nightmare, that's what it comes to.

TREPLEV: Yes, you should really live in town. [*Seeing* MASHA *and* MEDVEDENKO] Look here, you'll be told when the show begins, so don't hang round now. Go away, please.

SORIN: [*to* MASHA] Masha, would you mind asking your father to have that dog let off its chain? It's always howling. My sister couldn't sleep again last night.

MASHA: Speak to my father yourself, I shan't. Kindly leave me out of this. [*To* MEDVEDENKO] Come on.

MEDVEDENKO: [*to* TREPLEV] Let us know when it starts, will you? *Both go out.*

SORIN: So that dog will howl again all night. Isn't it typical? I've never done what I liked in the country. At one time I'd take a month off and come down here for a break and so on, but there'd be so much fuss and bother when you got here – you felt like pushing off the moment you arrived. [*Laughs.*] I was always glad to get away. Anyway, now I'm retired I've nowhere else to go, that's what it comes to. I have to live here, like it or not.

JACOB: [*to* TREPLEV] We're going for a swim, Mr Treplev.

TREPLEV: All right, but mind you're in your places in ten minutes. [*Looks at his watch.*] It won't be long now.

JACOB: Very good, sir.

[*Goes out.*]

TREPLEV: [*looking round the stage*] Well, this is our theatre. Just a curtain with the two wings and an empty space beyond. No scenery. There's an open view of the lake and horizon. We shall put up the curtain at exactly half past eight when the moon rises.

SORIN: Splendid.

TREPLEV: Of course the whole thing will fall flat if Nina Zarechny's late. It's time she was here. Her father and stepmother keep a sharp eye on her and she can't easily get away, she's pretty well a prisoner. [*Puts his uncle's tie straight.*] Your hair and beard are a mess. Shouldn't you get a trim?

SORIN: [*combing his beard*] It's the bane of my life. As a young man I always looked as if I had a hangover and so on. Women never liked me. [*Sitting down*] Why is your mother in a bad mood?'

Conversations in real life are often as complex as this, especially between people who know each other very well.

● Check the relationships between the characters then prepare this as a rehearsed reading. Try to work out what lies *beneath* what is being said.

For instance, does Sorin realise how ill he really is? Does he really think it is the country air that is upsetting him? Or does he fear something worse?

What is in Treplev's mind when he answers Sorin? Is he really listening to him?

Note that Jacob does not ask permission to go swimming: he simply tells Treplev that he is going.

In this way, it becomes clear that any spoken dialogue is rather like a chain of islands that appear separate but are connected below the water line. Sometimes people say what they think, no more, no less. At other times people say one thing while thinking something else. At yet other times people may be thinking and feeling, but saying nothing at all.

● Perform your group readings to each other and then discuss what underlies the ways in which the characters act and speak.

● When Nina is falling in love with Trigorin she has a scene in which he does most of the talking. What is she thinking during her silences? Write and perform a short monologue, 'The Silences of Nina'.

Stanislavsky is credited with saying that there are no small parts, only small actors. Test this statement by reference to one of the smallest parts in the play, the part of the Chef. The actor might be forgiven for thinking that

3c   Nina and Trigorin.

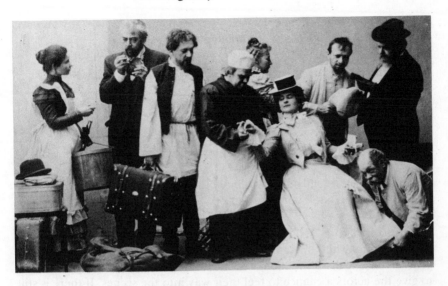

3d   The chef receives his tip.

the part is scarcely worth working upon because it is so tiny. This would not
have done for Stanislavsky, who would have pointed out that the actor must
do exactly the same as all the others in the play and use his imagination. He
should ask himself what he would feel like if he were a chef – particularly a
chef in Irene's household at the end of summer, when she goes away and
usually gives all the staff a tip. If he sets himself this sort of question and uses
his imagination to find acceptable answers then he will be on the road
towards creating a character, even though the part is a small one. He knows
that Irene is a bit of a skinflint, but he knows that he has done his job well and
she has been rather charming to him of late. Then he receives the shock of
discovering that the cook has been given a much larger tip. With all this in his
mind he should have a good idea of how to say his line, 'Oh thank you kindly,
madam. Have a pleasant journey. Thank you for your kindness.'

3.5   Rehearsing the scene

A number of legends have grown up around the rehearsal methods at the
Moscow Art Theatre. Most of them are exaggerations, but there is no doubt
that Stanislavsky's methods were very time-consuming. Every quest for
perfection inevitably takes time and seems over-fussy to people watching.

● Try applying these methods in a simplified form to your own rehearsals.

● Form groups so that each may concentrate on one of the acts, or
preferably one short scene or series of units within it.

You will find the methods explained in greater detail in Stanislavsky's books, especially *Creating a Role*. You should proceed as follows:

● Cast the characters.

● Give the actors time to work first on their own and then as a group to discuss where the *units* occur.

● For each unit find the *objectives* or motivations for each actor concerned.

● Set the scene roughly using ordinary furniture and stand-in props. Then walk through, book in hand.

As a result of the first walk-through, a number of questions and disagreements may have arisen. There will also be (indeed there *ought* to be) a general sense of dissatisfaction. Try one or two more read-throughs in order to give the actors a chance to feel their way into the scenes. If there is still dissatisfaction, then stop the rehearsal and discuss in terms of units and objectives. It may be necessary to concentrate on one unit for some time and then to run into it from the previous unit to see if it is now working reasonably well. If it is, go on to the following units of the act.

● Put the scripts down. Do not strain to remember the dialogue, but hold fast to your character and the motivations of that character.

● Now walk through the scene following the moves you have already worked out and *improvise* speeches and gestures that are suitable. The intention here is to give each actor confidence in himself and his colleagues and also to strengthen the connection between the inner emotion and the outer action.

● A further development of the previous stage is to walk the scene through, playing all the physical actions, but silently. Think the words but do not speak them. This is very difficult at first but comes with practice. You might like to discuss the reasons for this method.

● Then continue to rehearse in the normal way as long as time permits, but always try to resolve difficulties by the methods suggested above. At no point should your director demonstrate or in any way impose a performance upon you. Indeed, you may prefer to work as an ensemble, with no director at all.

You need not go so far as to learn all the words of your part but you may be pleasantly surprised to discover how near you are to complete memorisation after a few rehearsals. This will be because you have gone below the surface of the lines to explore the meaning.

● When you are ready, share your prepared readings in turn with the other groups. Play the whole play through and then discuss. It might help if all the actors who played the same character got together first to exchange notes.

● Take account of the criticisms of your colleagues and, if there is time, try again. Stanislavsky, according to legend, took months!

3.6 Realisation

If, in its own day, *The Seagull* was a challenge to the actors, the technical problems of mounting it on the stage would not have been considered particularly difficult, because any well-equipped theatre could provide facilities for four or five complete changes of scene in one evening. Nowadays, actors are no longer daunted by the style in which it is written. On the other hand, stage-managers prefer to have one permanent set.

To understand the play fully it is necessary to treat it as we have the others in this book with a study towards a complete realisation in the style that suits it best. Before we can solve the problems, we must see exactly what they are.

● Divide into four groups, one for each act of the play. Your first task is to prepare sketches for a ground plan of your chosen act. Presume for the moment that you would have as much space as you would need. If your act is set inside the house, decide exactly where the doors are and which side they are hinged. What windows there are whether they are curtained or not. What furniture? Where placed? What important props need to be provided? If your scene is exterior, consider where entrances will be and how they will be masked. What furniture is disposed around the set? Finally, what differences of levels could be introduced? What kind of backcloth will you need? How will it be lit to indicate time of day or period in the year?

● When you have finished your sketches, draw them out carefully on a scale agreed by all the groups preferably on transparent paper. You will then be able to superimpose your plans and to consider what practical problems might be created in the setting and striking of your scenes. You may well also be able to consider how these problems might have been solved in the professional theatre.

● Then by reference to the play itself and to the limitations of any possible acting-area, consider how you might achieve a minimum-resource realisation.

● Finally, do not overlook the time-interval between Acts Three and Four. How will this affect costumes? Will Masha continue to wear black after her marriage? What would it imply if she did? Does Treplev when he becomes a successful writer begin to dress like Trigorin? What other questions of this kind can be invented?

4
'The Importance of Being Earnest' by Oscar Wilde

The play was first produced at the St James's Theatre, London, on 14 February 1895 under the management of George Alexander, who played the part of John Worthing. The St James's stood in King Street, Westminster, from 1835 until 1957, when, in spite of a campaign to preserve it because of its architectural interest, it was demolished to be replaced by an office block. It was a typical Victorian theatre, with gallery, dress circle, stage boxes, pit and stalls arranged in a horseshoe pattern, with a proscenium arch and an orchestra pit.

Born in 1858, Alexander managed the theatre from 1891 until his death in 1918. Knighted in 1911, he was a typical London actor–manager of the kind that had existed since the Restoration. In most companies during all this time one man was responsible not only for playing the leading roles but also for commissioning playwrights and for artistic and financial policy in general.

Although the play was a great success, it had to be withdrawn before the run was over because of the scandal that grew around Wilde at the time of his trial. Later, when the controversy had cooled down, Alexander revived the play very successfully and it has remained in the repertoire of most major companies ever since. References are to *Five Plays* by Oscar Wilde (Penguin, 1969).

4a   John Worthing and Algernon, St. James's Theatre, 1909.

4.1   Barriers across the path

At first reading, this play seems to present few difficulties to the reader and
the performer might be forgiven for regarding it as easy to act. Neither
would have much trouble with the language, which is straightforward
nineteenth-century prose, obviously carefully designed to create certain
comic effects. The world it depicts, although artificial, seems in many ways
near enough to our own times to be recognisable and therefore easier to
re-create than Shakespeare's England. Furthermore, we might think that
the author has done half the work for us by setting up strong comic situations
and very witty punch lines so that all the performer has to do is to rehearse
the situation once or twice, learn and deliver the witticisms, collect the
laughs and so score an easy success.

However, the reader may find it necessary to be a little more precise in his definition of what he means by 'Victorian', while the actor may discover that comedy of any kind is very difficult to play. Alexander's company had no need to research into the 1890s. All they had to do was to polish their already shining technique. Today, we must not only practise and polish the technique but also first research the period.

Queen Victoria reigned for more than sixty years. The play was produced towards the end of that period. It is worthwhile looking at illustrated social-history books to get the feeling of the times. Changes in fashion tell us a lot about the people who followed them, but more importantly we need to understand what most people in the very first audience for the play understood and took for granted about such matters as the ownership of property, social class and the relationships between the sexes. (See also Chapters Three and Five.)

The last decade of Victoria's reign, the 1890s was regarded as a special time. The ending of the century was taken to indicate the ending of old ways of doing things, with a promise of fine new things to come. For some people, it was almost like approaching the end of the world, when anything could be permitted. The play itself is not only typically Victorian but typically *fin de siècle*. Its central theme is a guilty secret. Guilty secrets were central to many of the serious novels and plays of the time. Wilde himself had written such a play, *A Woman of No Importance*. This contains a very effective curtain line.

GERALD: [*he is quite beside himself with rage and indignation*] Lord Illingworth, you have insulted the purest thing on God's earth, a thing as pure as my own mother. You have insulted the woman I love most in the world with my own mother. As there is a God in Heaven, I will kill you!

MRS ARBUTHNOT: [*rushing across and catching hold of him*] No! No!

GERALD: [*thrusting her back*]. Don't hold me, mother. Don't hold me – I'll kill him!

MRS ARBUTHNOT: Gerald!

GERALD: Let me go, I say!

MRS ARBUTHNOT: Stop, Gerald, stop! He is your own father!

● Try this out, but beware of overdoing it. It deserves to be played quite seriously.

About this time Ibsen wrote *Ghosts*, which was about a guilty secret in one particular family but which was typical of many others (see Chapter Five). But in *The Imporance of Being Earnest* the secret around Jack Worthing only *seems* to be guilty.

In order further to accustom yourself to the style and language used in plays of the time read the following scene from *Mrs Dane's Defence* by

Henry Arthur Jones, first produced in 1900. The setting is '*The blue drawing-room at Lady Eastney's*'. Mr Risby, described as an ordinary Englishman of about thirty-five, is talking to his uncle and aunt, Mr and Mrs Bulsom-Porter.

MRS BULSOM-PORTER: [*looks at him very fixedly for a few moments*] No, Jim; I do not and cannot believe you.

RISBY: I'm sorry. However, the fact remains, my dear aunt, that I have inadvertently injured a very charming woman –

MRS BULSOM-PORTER: Of course! A very charming woman! That's the reason you withdraw your accusation.

RISBY: I made no accusation. And if you have repeated what I told you in the strictest confidence about Mrs Dane, I must beg you to put the matter right at once. For if you give me as your authority I shall have to explain that I was mistaken, that consequently you were mistaken, and further, that from this moment, you are fully aware that you are mistaken.

MRS BULSOM-PORTER: I'm not fully aware that I'm mistaken.

BULSOM-PORTER: What does it matter whether you're mistaken or no? Suppose Mrs Dane is Miss Hindemarsh, what then?

MRS BULSOM-PORTER: What then? Do you consider her fit to mix in the society of your wife?

BULSOM-PORTER: I daresay she's as fit as nine out of ten of the women you meet if the truth were only known. [*To Risby*] What was the exact story of this Miss Hindemarsh?

RISBY: Oh, the eternal trio! *Dramatis personae*, Mr Horace Trent, charming, devoted, middle-aged husband; Mrs Horace Trent, charming, devoted, middle-aged wife; Felicia Hindemarsh, charming, devoted, youthful governess to their children and companion to Mrs Trent; the whole forming a truly happy family, who passed the autumn at the Italian lakes, and returned by Vienna at the time I was an attaché there five years ago. During their stay in Vienna, charming, middle-aged wife discovers a liaison between charming, middle-aged husband and charming, youthful governess; and instead of sensibly packing off missy with a month's salary and saying no more about it, charming, middle-aged wife, being a neurotic creature, commits suicide. Charming, middle-aged husband is naturally horrified, and also refrains from doing the sensible thing – in fact, goes out of his mind, and is at present in an asylum in the north of England. Missy does the sensible thing and disappears. The story is hushed up as far as possible, but the moral remains: 'Upon the verge of such a tragedy may any one of us poor innocents be treading at this moment.' [*Takes out watch.*] Adieu, auntie. I have to catch an early train to town to-morrow morning.

MRS BULSOM-PORTER: You are sure Mrs Dane is not Miss Hindemarsh?

RISBY: Quite sure.

The Importance of Being Earnest *by Oscar Wilde*

Before starting work on this scene, notice the setting. Presumably her ladyship has more than one drawing-room in order for them to be distinguished by their colours. As for the language, we cannot be certain whether members of the English upper classes really spoke as polysyllabically and in such carefully balanced phrases as these characters do, but there is no doubt that in the novels and plays of the time they did!

● Form groups to prepare readings to share. The scene ends with the arrival of the mysterious Mrs Dane. Guess the reaction of each character.

● Now form small groups to prepare a short improvised scene for one of the following titles:

A Mother's Secret
A Father's Secret
The Butler's Secret
The Housemaid's Secret
Lady Mary's Secret
The Vicar's Secret

The scenes may be quite short but should be definitely set in the Victorian era and use the kind of dialogue used in *Mrs Dane's Defence.* Aim for comedy but be prepared to state what *kind* of comedy you were hoping to achieve.

It is most likely that at the first attempt you will use **burlesque**, because that is a natural reaction against the stiffness and artificiality that we think of as being typically Victorian. But what other kinds of comedy are there? Textbooks give us many definitions, but it might be more useful to share experiences of all the different television programmes that get lumped together as comedy and to attempt to classify them by noting their similarities and differences (see Glossary).

How would you classify *The Importance of Being Earnest*? Some people would call it a **farce**, others would say it is a **comedy of manners** or even a **comedy of character**.

4.2 Preparing for the task

The Victorian upper classes seem to have been drilled into good posture when quite young. Under the eyes of governesses, girls paraded schoolrooms with books balanced upon their heads. (Try it.) Boys were drilled in the army style: 'Stand up straight. Head up. Chest out, chin in, thumbs in line with the seams of the trousers.' (Try that, too.)

Refer to Chapter 3.2 for a detailed discussion on the relationship between posture and relaxation and the importance of both to the actor.

● For this particular play, try to assume the general Victorian upper-class posture, which was imitated, in a deferential sort of way, by servants.

Individual variations of posture are the first indication of character differences. For instance, Cecily has to be reminded by Lady Bracknell that 'Chins are being worn a little high this year', but Gwendolen will never need this advice. What habitual posture differences are there between both the younger women and Lady Bracknell? Between Jack and Algernon? Between Canon Chasuble and Miss Prism?

● Learn how to perform any simple conjuring trick which depends upon nimbleness of the fingers; practise it and then teach it to somebody else. Also, improve the patter that goes with it so that the intended effect is achieved in time and in rhythm with the words spoken. This is a basic skill for an actor in high-quality farce.

The handling of props, particularly items of clothing, the eating of food, the consumption of drink must be carefully timed and rehearsed.

● As a group exercise set up a social function to involve the whole company as hosts, servants and guests. The activities of entering, being relieved of outdoor clothes by servants, greetings, eating and drinking should be accurately mimed and timed. Conversation, need not be improvised in the form of intelligible words. Instead, use one or two stock phrases from the period, such as 'greenery–yallery' and 'Grosvenor Gallery', which can be spoken with a variety of intonations at the whim of the speaker to convey the small change of conversation. (The phrases come from W. S. Gilbert, who **satirised** Wilde in the opera *Patience*.)

● Now apply your skill, in groups of four or five, to a walk-through of the action in Act One, immediately following Jack's first entrance. Before speaking the lines, plot all the movements, down to the last detail. For instance, does Lane take Jack's hat and coat and cane, if any? Does Jack take off his gloves, if any? Where is Algernon standing? How far from the door? How many sandwiches does he eat? Next, one actor walks through John's movements and another actor speaks the lines. This obviates the difficulty that arises from having to move and act with a script in your hands. The same can be done for Algernon. This is a workshop practice technique rather than one to be used at rehearsals.

Once scenes like this have been rehearsed up to the point of reasonable smoothness, the actors may begin to modify what they do in order to bring

4b   The *Patience* Cartoon.

out character differences. For instance, in the two eating-sequences in the play Jack has a different style from Algernon.

Building up to and getting a good laugh from an audience calls for the same skills used in passing a ball rapidly from one to another until it reaches the striker who scores the goal.

● Before rehearsals, warm up by actually throwing a ball from one person to another around the cast. Do not try to surprise each other but aim fair and catch crisply. Then take a piece of dialogue and speak the lines as you throw the ball to the person who must answer. Do not aim for speed, aim for accuracy. Think of giving and receiving your cues. Do not think of throwing the cue *at* a fellow actor but of thowing *to* him. There may be one or two moments when it may seem that the writer intends the line to be thrown hard at the recipient in order to demolish him, but we must

55

remember that it is the *character* who is to be demolished. The actor, while appearing to suffer humiliation, is actually playing his part in the game very calmly and efficiently.

● Practise the following dialogue. (Sir Peter Teazle, an old bachelor, has married a young wife. She is beautiful but extravagant.)

> SIR PETER: . . . I have made you a woman of fashion, of fortune, of rank – in short, I have made you my wife.
>
> LADY TEAZLE: Well, then, and there is but one thing more you can make me to add to the obligation, that is –
>
> SIR PETER: My widow, I suppose?
>
> LADY TEAZLE: Hem! hem!
>
> SIR PETER: I thank you, madam – but don't flatter yourself; for, though your ill-conduct may disturb my peace of mind, it shall never break my heart, I promise you: however, I am equally obliged to you for the hint.
>
> LADY TEAZLE: Then why will you endeavour to make yourself so disagreeable to me, and thwart me in every little elegant expense?
>
> SIR PETER: 'Slife, madam, I say, had you any of these little elegant expenses when you married me?
>
> LADY TEAZLE: Lud, Sir Peter! would you have me be out of the fashion?
>
> SIR PETER: The fashion, indeed! what had you to do with the fashion before you married me?
>
> LADY TEAZLE: For my part, I should think you would like to have your wife thought a woman of taste.
>
> SIR PETER: Ay – there again – taste! Zounds! madam, you had no taste when you married me!
>
> LADY TEAZLE: That's very true, indeed, Sir Peter!

This exchange, from Sheridan's *School for Scandal*, is a duel but also a game. They are really fond of each other, so there is no spite in it.

The first rule for any actor appearing in comedy is 'Never *try* to be funny'. Trying too hard to make a line funny drives the actor to the use of a comic voice, a funny face, or absurd and exaggerated gesture. In comedy, as in all other drama, the aim must be to create a character moving and acting in a situation. Usually the character is not aware that he is funny, so the actor's job is to find out why he acts in this strange way which is funny to other people. In short, do not ask 'How?', ask 'Why?'

A comic role must be prepared as seriously as any other. There is no special 'comedy technique'. Any experienced actor will say that the only difference between **comedy** and **tragedy** is that comedy is much harder to play.

● Practise speech skills in every possible way. Choose examples from Shakespeare to the moderns. Read and speak Hamlet's advice to the players (see Chapter One). Try the extract from *The Bear* in Chapter Three. Then you will be ready to work upon the dialogue of this highly sophisticated comedy. Above all, resist the temptation to take a short cut by imitating the way in which any great actor may have spoken the lines.

4.3 Exploring the background

Shaw wrote, 'There are no social problems. What is wrong with the poor is poverty. What is wrong with the rich is idleness.' Even servants in this play had privileges beyond the wildest dreams of most of the people in England at that time. All the principal characters are, by any standards, remarkably rich, and so not seem to have to work for their income.

● Refer to social history and, in particular, to bound volumes of *Punch* for further details of the fashionable pastimes, topics of conversation and general preoccupations of the people who lived in the 1890s.

Of course, fashions change and the very upper crust of society would never dream of becoming unfashionable by clinging too long to certain pursuits, which in any case would become imitated by their social inferiors, and thus, in the strict sense of the word, *common*.

● When you have completed your researches, put together an 1890s after-dinner evening party. Look up the etiquette, particularly with reference to table manners. Consider what would have been on the menu, but concentrate more on what would have taken place after the meal had been cleared away and everybody had adjourned to the drawing-room. Every member of the party must contribute to the general enjoyment and edification of the rest, by singing a song, reciting a poem or organising a game.

Songs of the time tended to be sentimental or patriotic, at least among the genteel classes. The working classes were also sentimental and patriotic but enjoyed outspokenly bawdy songs.

Some of the younger guests rather influenced by new ideas might well attempt to start a discussion about the Condition of Women, but most of the company at a typical evening party of the period preferred to play games. These were of two kinds. Some were very active, indeed boisterous. *Blind Man's Buff*, for instance, was popular with the young of both sexes because it permitted more free personal physical contact than was permitted by strict etiquette. Other games, sometimes organised by the Miss Prisms of the company, contained a strong element of self-improvement. These included spelling-bees, and what we should now call quizzes. Also, *Consequences*, charades and *tableaux vivants*. These 'living pictures' were derived not from the 'decadent' art of Wilde's friends, such as Aubrey Beardsley and James McNeill Whistler, but from the safe and respected Academy painters, whose pictures always told a story. These illustrated incidents from history (*When Did You Last See Your Father?*), or a scene from Shakespeare (Portia taunting Shylock), or, most popularly, a scene which not only told a story but also pointed a moral: *Forgiveness Awaits the Penitent Sinner*. These could be in one or two scenes, complementary or contrasting, and, while generally held in still poses, could sometimes dramatically come to life.

4.4   Characters and relationships

In Chapter Three reference is made to the theories of Stanislavsky and the deep study required for the actor to understand the character he is to play. At first sight it would seem that Stanislavsky's advice is not very useful to the actor faced with the task of creating such a character as John Worthing or Lady Bracknell. If the plot is as highly improbable as this one, then one might expect that the characters will be distorted to fit it. This sort of play, like much eighteenth- and nineteenth- century comedy, may be best played more technically than psychologically.

● Form small groups, one for each character. Perhaps you could deal with the two menservants in one group in order to make sure that you get an effective contrast between them.

● Concentrate on the *facts* that Wilde has provided. The number of these will vary from character to character.

We are told a great deal about John Worthing, including his politics. Some of these facts enable us to make further deductions. For instance, a man who can afford more than one residence is likely to be comfortably off. The fact that he is a Justice of the Peace indicates that he is accepted as being respectable.

We are given fewer facts about Lady Bracknell, so the actress playing the part has greater room for experiment. Great parts attract great performers and great performers tend to leave their stamp upon a part. Sometimes their interpretations differ. When Judi Dench played the part that had previously been played by Edith Evans, she made Lady Bracknell younger than Evans did, and much more friendly to Algernon. Having seen a performance of a **classic**, refer to the text as soon as possible afterward in order to decide how much of what you saw came from the writer and how much from the actor.

The Importance of Being Earnest *by Oscar Wilde*

4c   Gwendolen, Algernon and Lady Bracknell.

● Expand the groups to consider characters in relationship with each other. If Wilde's characters continued to exist after the final curtain as Chekhov's were supposed to do, then how might they behave in the following circumstances?

Suppose Cecily and Gwendolen have agreed to have a double wedding. How would they go about suggesting this to Aunt Augusta, who may not be likely to approve?

After their own marriage, how might Miss Prism set about reforming Canon Chasuble's somewhat disorganised lifestyle?

Suppose that the two young couples have been married for some time. Set up a situation in which they have their first quarrel. What is it about? Who wins?

4d   Miss Prism and Mr Chasuble, Old Vic Theatre, 1934.

● Invent other improvisations in order to explore the characters further. Do not forget minor characters. For instance, what exactly was the misunderstanding that led Lane into his marriage with the young person? In every case you may be inventive but you must never contradict the information provided by the writer.

4.5   Rehearsing the scene

The play is in three acts. Each of these can be divided, for rehearsal purposes, into a series of short scenes or sequences. The construction is artificial, with exits and entrances arranged for the convenience of the plot rather than any plausible motivation of the characters. The main aim throughout is to achieve comic theatrical effects. This in one way makes rehearsals simpler to organise, because the director can take a sequence at a time and work upon it separately from all the others.

● First, make a synopsis for each sequence. For instance, the first sequence of Act One is an introductory one establishing certain facts, which might be summarised as follows: Algernon is a wealthy young bachelor, living in a flat in the West End of London. He is attended by a manservant and is expecting a visit from his aunt, Lady Bracknell, for tea.

● Next, seek to encapsulate the action and mood of the sequence in as few words as possible, and to make a link with the next sequence. For instance: Algernon has a friend called Jack, who lives in the country and has come to London to propose to Gwendolen, but Algernon objects to the marriage because of Cecily . . . .

If you can manage to tell the whole story without every coming to a full stop and not using 'and' too often you will be aware of the *logical sequence* which, although quite ridiculous, is the backbone of the play.

Awareness of this structure will save the actors the strain of trying desperately to make every funny line earn its laugh. Not all the lines are directly connected with the plot; nor do they all arise from the basic **themes.** Some lines should be played in the hope of making the audience laugh in the same way that a bowler in a cricket match is hoping to get the batsman out every time he delivers the ball, but laugh lines which are also plot lines or theme lines *must* hit the wicket.

Once director and cast have made sure of the flow of the main impetus of the plot, they can begin to look in detail at each sequence to see where the most important comic lines occur.

Let us consider the very first scene. It presents a problem to a contemporary director, because theatre-going habits were markedly different in 1890 from today. Wilde, and his producer, George Alexander, knew that the audience at the St James's expected to be given time to have a good look at the set and perhaps even applaud it before settling down to enjoy the play. Another convention of the time was that the leading actor seldom appeared at the very beginning of the play, and since Alexander was playing Jack there would have been a page and a half of dialogue before he made an entrance. So the modern director would be advised not to try to start the play on a high note.

However, the actor playing Lane (who might also have been an understudy to both principal men) is not too badly served with Wildean lines which give the audience a foretaste of the sort of entertainment being offered. He has a speech which helps to set the period atmosphere well: 'I have only been married once. That was in consequence of a misunderstanding between myself and a young person.' But there is an earlier exchange which, in addition to setting off a sequence of laughs, calls attention to one of the basic themes of the play – marriage:

ALGERNON: Why is it that in a bachelor's establishment the servants invariably drink the champagne? I ask merely for information.

LANE: I attribute it to the superior quality of the wine, sir. I have observed that in married households the champagne is rarely of a first rate brand.

ALGERNON: Good heavens! Is marriage so demoralising as that?

When Algernon asks this question he is making a reference sure to get a laugh from an audience who knew about such things; but which word takes the main stress: 'bachelor's', 'servants', 'invariably', 'drink' or 'champagne'? Also, what is the general tone of the question? In real life at those times it could have been a very serious matter for Lane if his master had been really angry about this, but this is a comedy. Algernon reassures Lane with his next remark: 'I ask merely for information.' This has given Lane time to think his way out of it (characters in comedy frequently need time for this purpose) and to reply, with just a touch of flattery, 'I have often observed that in married households the champagne is rarely of a first rate brand.' How does Lane stress this line? Fairly obviously, the important word is 'married', because this leads naturally into Algernon's line 'Good heavens! Is marriage so demoralising as that?' We can now be quite sure how Algernon's original question should be stressed: obviously at 'bachelor's', in order to connect with the theme word 'marriage'.

It could be argued that this process is over-analytical and that good actors will find their way intuitively towards the right intonations. This is only half true, and in any case there will be times when intuition may fail. The actor must always keep in mind the connection between the individual line, and the general tone of the play. A line may carry several layers of meaning, and in *The Importance of Being Earnest* there is a surprisingly large number of lines which if spoken with the wrong intonation may destroy the atmosphere. For instance, if Algernon appeared to be *genuinely* concerned for the health of Mr Bunbury, then we should lose the total heartlessness without which the comedy could not work.

The first Wildean epigram in the play is given to Algernon. He must decide whether this is to be spoken as **soliloquy** or **direct address** (see Glossary), but whatever he does with the line he must make quite sure that he has cleared the audience's view for Jack's entrance. Entrances (such as Lady Bracknell's in Act One and Miss Prism's in Act Three) are frequently very important in comedy and can be very funny in themselves, if properly contrived. All entrances in farcical comedy should be perfectly visible to the audience, even if they do seem contrived.

To return to Act One, the dialogue following Jack's first entrance must proceed at a good pace and must be rehearsed for timing and prop-handling (see Unit 2). The scene is mainly exposition, light comedy rather than farce.

A good actor can certainly use the line 'And very good bread and butter it is too' to indicate Jack's yearning love for Gwendolen and thus help Algernon to start the plot moving again with the line 'I don't think you ever will be.'

4.6 Realisation

If a production of this play was being prepared, it would be interesting to use the research already done to achieve the utmost historical authenticity, but it would cost a lot. A production 'in the round' would retain authenticity of costume but reduce the funishings to an absolute minimum. This would raise some interesting problems in grouping, but you would be able to create an intimate atmosphere so that your actors could share the humour with the audience rather than have to project it at them.

● Try some scenes in each form and compare the effects.

● Compile a list of furniture and properties as for a proscenium arch production, then go through it deleting every item which is not absolutely essential. The remaining items would be used if you were working in the round.

(See Unit 6 of other chapters for further suggestions towards realisation.)

5
'Ghosts' by Henrik Ibsen

Written in 1881, the play was first produced in Norwegian in Chicago in 1882. It was first performed in England in 1891 by the Independent Theatre Society, directed by Jack Grein, at the Royalty Theatre, London. The translator was William Archer, who did much with Bernard Shaw to enhance Ibsen's reputation, in the face of bitter attacks from some critics.

References are to Henrik Ibsen, *Four Major Plays*, translated by J. McFarlane (Oxford University Press, 1981).

5.1 Barriers across the path

When this play was first produced it immediately aroused a storm of controversy because it dealt with the then-unmentionable subject of inherited venereal disease. The name of Henrik Ibsen has become highly respected, but there may still be a very large number of people who would not pay to go and see this play. Neither would they switch on television to see it. This would not necessarily be because of the subject matter itself. The average playgoer might admire Ibsen as a social reformer but equally shy away from his plays, especially this one. He might offer several reasons for doing this.

The play is merely propaganda and propaganda can never be entertaining

This is not true. Bertolt Brecht, who always wrote from a committed political stance, is on record as having said, 'A theatre that cannot be laughed in is a

64

Ghosts *by Henrik Ibsen*

5a   Edvard Munch's sketch for Max Reinhardt's production, Berlin 1906.

theatre to be laughed at.' Dario Fo, the author of many political plays, is one of the finest comedians working in the theatre today. It is true that propaganda drama (or should we call it didactic drama?) is very difficult to write. To prove this statement try the following apparently simple task.

● Form small groups to prepare and present a two-minute TV 'commercial' on behalf of an anti-smoking group or road safety lobby or similar organisation. Then discuss the difficulties.

The main story line is incredible

● First of all make sure that you know the main story line. Revise it quickly by dividing into three groups, one for each act, noting the main events. Then compare this story with any you know of in any other drama, especially classic tragedy, Greek or Shakespearean. Then consider whether or not some news items in the popular press are not equally incredible!

There are long passages of dialogue in which nothing happens

This is more true than some of the other objections. There are seven pages of duologue between Pastor Manders and Mrs Alving in Act One. The question as to whether or not anything 'happens' depends upon the skill of the actors. Their task can be made easier by judicious cutting.

● Form a 'standing committee' for cutting the play. As you work through the play you may well come across long speeches or even complete passages of dialogue which somebody may feel could be cut without harming the general effect of the play. These speeches could be presented to the cutting-committee, who would have to decide on the merits of the case in the light of the demands of plot, character and atmosphere.

Some speeches, though long, are impossible to cut. Consider the following:

MRS ALVING: I'll tell you what I mean. The reason I'm so timid and afraid is that I can never get properly rid of the ghosts that haunt me.

MANDERS: What did you call them?

MRS ALVING: Ghosts. When I heard Regine and Oswald in there, it was just like seeing ghosts. But then I'm inclined to think that we are all ghosts, Pastor Manders, every one of us. It's not just what we inherit from our mothers and fathers that haunts us. It's all kinds of old defunct theories, all sorts of old defunct beliefs, and things like that. It's not that they actually *live* on in us; they are simply lodged there, and we cannot get rid of them. I've only to pick up a newspaper and I seem to see ghosts gliding between the lines. Over the whole country there must be ghosts, as numerous as the sands of the sea. And here we are, all of us, abysmally afraid of the light.

It is worth noting that some translators use 'dead' instead of 'defunct'. Which word is better for the actor?

● Try speaking the speech aloud aiming to bring out the depth of meaning.

The language is artificial; it also suffers from the process of translation

This does not seem to apply to the speech above, but it is true that what is beautiful poetry in one language may appear rather clumsy and even prosaic when translated into another. Ibsen gave up writing in verse some years before *Ghosts*, but continued his work in 'heightened prose'. This is a convention similar to that still existing today of writing in blank verse or rhyme. It is merely a matter of deciding what convention is to be followed and then making it clear to the audience. The actor must not only accept the convention but use it for its advantages. Mrs Alving's speech quoted above needs to be treated with the same care and skill as Shakespearean verse, especially in phrasing and appreciation of the rhythms.

Language is also used to underline complexities and contradictions within characters. Engstrand, for instance, uses language as a mask. This is an interesting challenge for the actor.

● Find examples and try playing the scenes in which he does this.

Once a translator has arrived at a satisfactory version of one of the more overtly poetic speeches in such a play, he can rest assured that it will be useful for a very long time. It is the more colloquial and mundane passages which are likely to wear thin by rapidly becoming out of date.

● Set up another standing committee, this time concerned with tidying up the translation. It is comparatively easy to spot the lines that are not quite right, but very difficult to find good substitutes. Beware of becoming too up-to-date, in case the fashion changes too quickly, and bear in mind the differences between true period speech and the merely quaint.

The characters are not true to life

This is fair comment. Engstrand's deformity, which would nowadays be called a disability, is too obviously symbolic of his wickedness. Pastor Manders appears to a modern audience more comic than Ibsen intended him to be. Oswald talks and behaves rather too much like a bohemian young artist. These are difficulties to be overcome by competent acting and sensitive direction. When we come to consider characterisation we must remember to look for the truth being represented, not for errors in the drawing.

The objector might conclude with a generalisation of anti-Ibsenism such as 'The very opening of the play in that dull middle class room with the gloomy landscape outside half obscured by steady rain is enough to drive anybody out of the theatre.' We could reply that the beginning is deliberately low-key and that good design and stage-management can create an ending which will combine poetic speech with visual beauty to evoke the emotions of pity and terror. That is what great **tragedy** is supposed to be about.

5.2 Preparing for the task

This is a play of ideas, expressed both in words and action. Physical action is more important in this play than many people think, but let us begin with the words and consider how they should be spoken.

One of the first jobs of the actor is to get the words off the printed page into his own mind and then out through his mouth. It is very difficult to understand a complex idea when it is set out in print. It is far better to hear it spoken. Best of all is to hear it spoken in one's own voice. In this way the actor is made to feel that the sense and feeling are his own. Unfortunately, it is at precisely this stage that the difficulties arise.

If you really want to understand the text of any play, try the following experiment.

5b   Regina Engstrand, The Greenwich Theatre, 1974.

● Go somewhere where you can be private and make a tape recording of any speech that puzzles you. Do not try to make this into a performance. Do not aim for characterisation. Do not aim to do anything other than to make sense of what you are saying.

● Play the recording back and see if you understand what you have said. If the passage is really difficult then you will have the experience of hearing yourself talking what seems to be incomprehensible rubbish, but don't despair. This happens frequently to professional actors when they are taking the first steps towards learning a classic part.

Many people read too quickly, especially when reading silently. Drama is meant to be spoken. The very first line of the play, if spoken in one breath, will come out like this:

Whatdoyouwantstaywhereyouareyouaredrippingwet

Even on the page it has lost much of its meaning, because it has lost its *shape*. Even if it is divided into three sentences equally spaced for breath –

What do you want Stay where you are You are dripping wet

– it will still carry very little meaning, and if it is read on one note all the time it will carry no feeling either (although this is preferable to the meaningless switchbacking tone practised by some elocutionists determined to display their vocal skills at all costs).

Now let us concentrate on one of the sentences:

What do you want?

This has now got its punctuation mark to indicate that it is a question. It seems simple enough, but it will still remain meaningless until the speaker takes the trouble to look beyond the words into the *situation* in which they are spoken.

Every word spoken on the stage must be spoken so that the audience can hear it, but we must also remember that every word spoken on the stage is addressed to somebody else. Unless the actor is in **soliloquy** or using direct address, he is talking to another person on the stage. So whom is Regine talking to? It is Engstrand, her supposed father, whom she hates and who has no business in the house. Once the actress knows this there is no more difficulty with the first sentence of this line. She just speaks the line as she herself might speak to somebody she did not like who was trying to get into a place which was her own domain. The actor might very well stress the word 'you' as in everyday life. The next two sentences can be treated in much the same way. These simple rules will help actors deal with longer and more complex speeches.

It has been presumed so far that the whole line could be taken on one breath, which is physically quite easy, or it could be split into three separate sentences, but there are other possible variations in the pattern. Regine could say,

What do you want? Stay where you are. . . . You're dripping wet.

Or she could say,

What do you want? . . . Stay where you are! You're dripping wet.

There are other possible patterns. Try experimenting with them. Although this may seem to be taking more trouble than such a simple line is worth, there is a very important lesson to be learnt here. How does the actress decide whether to pause in her speech and, if so, when and why?

There are two factors which control phrasing. The first is breathing. This depends upon your physical equipment and the amount of practice you do. (See Booklist for technical suggestions.) The second factor is imagination. The ultimate artistic effect will depend upon how far you are able to see the other character through the eyes of your own. It will therefore follow naturally that what you say will depend not only on how you speak your lines but also upon the other character's reaction to them.

For instance, does Regina shout her first sentence through the closed door at Engstrand? Does she expect him to stay outside? (There may be a rule forbidding him to enter the private part of the house.) She may open the door, in which case he may try to come in. She then says, 'Stay where you are!' in order to hold him off. Then in explanation, with some contempt for his stupidity, she might add, 'You're dripping wet!'

● Try the first three or four lines in pairs and take Hamlet's advice: 'Suit the word to the action, the action to the word.' (See Chapter One.)

● Practise saying, 'You can't do that. They won't let you. It's impossible anyway' in as many different ways as you can. Do not think of it as being a line from a tragedy, comedy, melodrama or whatever. Instead, imagine the circumstances in which somebody might say it to someone else. Try to achieve at least five different renderings, and hope that your listeners will be able to guess some of the circumstances.

Once you have experimented in this way, you will begin to appreciate the importance of punctuation to the actor. The full stop, the comma and the semicolon all have different, if not very precise, time values. (Test this by reading aloud.)

Pauses are almost as important to the actor as his words. A pause is not a blank. It should be filled with action, mental or physical. (Harold Pinter became famous for his use of pauses, but that may be simply because he took the trouble to write them in for his actors.)

● A good actor will work with his director to place pauses where they are most effective; try this on scenes from the play.

● Return to your own tape recordings and listen to them again, this time to consider the speed with which you spoke the lines.

Audiences may become alienated from an actor simply because he speaks too fast or too slow. Sometimes an actor thinks that the words are so important or beautiful, especially the way that he speaks them, that he tends to linger over them much longer than he should. If words are important or beautiful then they will remain so if taken at a natural pace. Over-rapid speech comes when the actor, perhaps out of nervousness, is literally just not thinking what he is saying. There is a simple rule that says, the more information you are giving the audience, the more you are likely to need to slow down. This is especially true at the beginning of the play, where there is likely to be a lot of exposition. The audience are given the facts they need to know together with hints of interesting things to come.

Try the following passage between Engstrand and Regine:

Ghosts *by Henrik Ibsen*

ENGSTRAND: . . . Now don't be such a fool as to stand in your own way, Regine. What can you do with yourself out here? Is it going to be any use to you, all this education the lady's lavished on you? You'll be looking after the children in the new Orphanage, they tell me. What sort of thing is that for a girl like you, eh? Are you all that keen on working yourself to death for the sake of a lot of dirty little brats?

REGINE: No, if things worked out as *I* wanted them to . . . Well, it could happen. It could happen!

ENGSTRAND: What could happen?

REGINE: Never you mind . . .

● Apply the suggestions given so far and this time bring the passage to life by considering what each character is *thinking* but not *saying*. Why does Engstrand want her to leave Mrs Alving? Why does she wish to stay?

Naturalistic dialogue should sound natural, which means that you need not wait for the other character to answer you before you speak again. On the page speeches must be separated for the convenience of the reader, but at times speeches tumble out across each other as in the following passage between Manders and Regine.

MANDERS: But a daughter's duty, my good girl. . . Of course we'd have to get the consent of your mistress first.

REGINE: But I'm not sure it's quite the thing for me, at my age, to keep house for a single man.

MANDERS: What! But my dear Miss Engstrand, we happen to be talking about your own father.

REGINE: Yes, that may be, but all the same. . . . Now, if it was in a *good* house with a proper gentleman. . .

MANDERS: But my dear Regine . . .

REGINE: . . . Somebody I could feel affection and respect for, and be a sort of daughter to . . .

MANDERS: Yes, but my dear, good child . . .

REGINE: Then I should be quite happy to go back to town. It's awfully lonely out here . . . and you know well enough yourself, Pastor, what it's like to be alone in the world. And I think I can honestly say I'm both willing and able. You don't know of any place like that for me, Pastor, do you?

MANDERS: Who, me? No, to be quite honest, I don't.

REGINE: But dear, dear Pastor Manders . . . you will think of me, won't you, if ever . . .

MANDERS: [*gets up*] Yes, that I will, Miss Engstrand.

REGINE: Because if I . . .

MANDERS: Would you be so kind as to fetch Mrs Alving?

REGINE: I'll see to it at once, Pastor.

71

● Play this through book in hand but also try to get the feel of the action. Regine is pursuing Manders rather harder than he wishes, so how does he respond?

Clive Barker, in his book *Theatre Games*, introduces a technique to help the actor to get at the thought behind the words by using a system of questioning to break up the actor's thought patterns into demand and response. To use Barker's own words (using as an example the opening speech of *Twelfth Night*, 'If music be the food of love . . .'):

> To start with, another actor supplies the questions. Later it is easy to do it for oneself. Thus:
>
> If (what?) Music.
> If <u>Music</u> (what?) be.
> If <u>Music</u> be (what?) the food.
> If <u>Music</u> be the <u>food</u> (food of what?) of Love.
> If <u>Music</u> be the <u>food</u> of <u>Love</u>, (what shall I do?) Give me.
> If <u>Music</u> be the <u>food</u> of <u>Love</u>, play on, <u>Give</u> me (what shall I give you?) <u>excess</u> of it.
>
> The words I have underlined are where the process produces the strongest kinaesthetic response in me; they therefore take the major stresses. It may be different for others. The alternatives are not infinite, but they are there. Each must find his own way.

Many of the longer speeches in this play can be treated in this way. Here is an example using one of Manders's speeches in Act One. M stands for Manders's original speech and Q for the questioner, helping the actor to arrive at the thought process.

> M. All your . . .
> Q. All your what?
> M. All your <u>life</u> you've always been . . .
> Q. Always been what?
> M. . . . quite disastrously <u>selfish</u> . . .

● Apply the technique to the whole speech and arrive at a pattern of stresses.

If you look back over the examples you will see how attention is called to the links in the chain of thought, thus making it easier for the actor to know not only what the character is saying but also how he thinks. After a time it is possible to be your own questioner. With practice you will find that if there is any sense at all in a speech this process will help you to tease it out. It will also, as Barker points out, give you a pattern of major stresses marking the rhythms of your speech. This is a useful tool for working upon obscure passages in Shakespeare.

Every play has a pattern of movement parallel to the pattern of speech. Sometimes the story is told in speech and movement; sometimes by one without the other. Sometimes what takes place in silence is more important than anything that is actually spoken. Are there any silent moments in this play which are especially telling in their effect?

Such effects do not have to be spectacular. Consider two moments in Act One. Manders when he first enters leaves his hat and bag on a chair. Left alone, he walks up and down the room, looks out of the window, comes back to the table and notices the books. When he sees the title page of one of them he gives a start. Mrs Alving enters and he turns to greet her. For the moment he has forgotten the books in his pleasure at meeting her again, but it is not long before they come to his attention and he feels that he must ask her about them.

● Prepare the scene in terms of speech, movement and character from the time that Manders is first left alone in the room to the moment he asks his question about the books. It may be necessary to invent actions which are not printed in the text. How do they greet each other? With warmth on her side? But what reaction from him? When does Mrs Alving sit down? Manders is presumably such a stickler for etiquette that he would not have seated himself if she were left standing. Any action you introduce must be true to its period and place. You should work out movements not merely to tell the story but to suggest the everyday habitual reality of the

5c   Mrs Alving, Regina Engstrand and Oswald Alving.

time and place. Mrs Alving is at home here. She moves through this room every day. Manders knew the place in the past but now returns after many years as a stranger. How do you show this?

The general atmosphere of *Ghosts* is one of growing tension. Actors must learn how to remain relaxed 'inside' their characters, however tense those characters must appear to be, (see Chapter 3.2 for a discussion on the need for physical relaxation and its relation to other acting-skills).

● Now repeat the process for other scenes, thinking all the time of patterns of movement to counterpoint the pattern of language. If you are interested in movement and dance, take the outline of the plot or concentrate upon one facet of it. Devise a dance-drama. You could extend the 'ghost' theme by introducing the ghosts of Captain Alving and Mrs Engstrand, watching over the action. Perhaps trying to intervene?

5.3   Exploring the background

● Refer to the previous chapter for reassurance that not all life in Europe at this time was as drab and gloomy as it is depicted in this particular play. Read *The Importance of Being Earnest*, refer to bound volumes of *Punch*, seek out and enjoy some of the lighter reading of the time. Above all, play some of the games described in Chapter 4.3

● George Alexander appeared in domestic drama as well as in comedy, but what might he have thought if he had been asked to appear in *Ghosts*? Set up a scene in which he is interviewed by a dramatic critic or, if you wish to explore the background even further, imagine what he might have said about Ibsen in a conversation with Bernard Shaw.

We tend nowadays to feel rather superior to the Victorians, but this may lead us to make unfair judgements. So complete was the conspiracy of silence about sexual matters that educated people in particular, unless they had studied medicine, had literally no language to use for discussion. The working classes and men of the upper class would have known the common expressions but middle class ladies had hardly any vocabulary except for a series of euphemisms.

● Set up a situation in which a character from *The Importance of Being Earnest*, Canon Chasuble, attempts to explain the plot of *Ghosts* to his newly married wife, previously Miss Prism the governess. This could be highly amusing but also rather sad.

It was at about this time that the science of psychology was turning its attention to the darker side of the human mind, especially the European human mind. It was discovered that there was a connection between folk tales, dreams and human sexuality. Ibsen must have realised this when he was writing his early poetic comedy *Peer Gynt.* In the following extract from Act Two in the Christopher Fry translation, Peer, now an outcast from his village, his clothes in tatters, is still defiant. He has been boasting at the top of his voice to the empty air. He takes a step forward, trips over a rock, falls and hits his head. And then, in his vision . . .

WOMAN IN GREEN. Is it true?

PEER: (*drawing his finger across his throat*)
  As true as my name is Peer;
  As true as you're a beautiful woman!
  Will you have me? You'll see how well I turn out;
  You needn't weave, you needn't spin,
  You can eat so much you'll give at the seams.
  What's more, I won't drag you about by the hair.

WOMAN IN GREEN: Nor beat me, either?

PEER: Now is that likely?
        Kings' sons don't go around beating women.

WOMAN IN GREEN: Are you a king's son?

PEER: Yes, I am.

WOMAN IN GREEN: And I am the King of the Dovre's daughter.

PEER: Really? Well, there's a happy coincidence.

WOMAN IN GREEN: His place is deep in the Ronde mountain.

PEER: My mother's is grander, I should say.

WOMAN IN GREEN: Do you know my father? King Brosse, his name is.

PEER: Do you know my mother? Her name's Queen Aase.

WOMAN IN GREEN: When father's angry, the mountains crack open.

PEER: They belch if my mother so much as grumbles.

WOMAN IN GREEN: My father can kick to the top of the roof-tree.

PEER: My mother can ride through a river in flood.

WOMAN IN GREEN: Are those rags the only clothes you've got?

PEER: Ah, you should see my Sunday outfit!

WOMAN IN GREEN: I wear silk and gold every day of the week.

PEER: It looks to me like shoddy and straw.

WOMAN IN GREEN: Yes, but you've got to bear in mind
  In my country everything we own
  Has two different ways of being looked at.
  If ever you visit my father's house
  At first you might believe you stood
  In a wilderness of scattered stones.

PEER: Extraordinary; it's the same with us.
  You'll think our gold is dirt and trash;
  You may even imagine the sparkling windows
  Are stuffed up with old stockings and rags.

WOMAN IN GREEN: Black can be white, and the ugly beautiful.
PEER: Big can seem little, and filth seem clean.
WOMAN IN GREEN: (*throwing her arms round his neck*).
   Oh, Peer, I can see we were made for each other.

5.4 Characters and relationships

'Mrs Alving looks like my Aunt Kate except that she's older and more educated but she's tall and thin, she has very strong hands and a quiet voice and when she loses her temper there's something a little bit mad about her eyes. They're blue.' This is the way that some people make up word-pictures about characters in fiction. You may not agree with it in every detail but you could use it as a model to invent your own descriptions for each of the characters in the play. Be prepared to justify what you say.

Some professional actors when called upon to create a new role consciously look around at people they meet, borrowing a habit of speech from one person and a way of walking from somebody else. One famous comic character in the thirties was a more or less complete portrait of one of the stagehands in the theatre where the play was produced. According to legend, he never recognised himself. Do you happen to know anybody who, physically at least, resembles your idea of Pastor Manders or any other character in the play?

5d Mrs Alving and Oswald Alving.

A famous actress once said that she always created her characters by thinking about what they would wear, by actually looking around the shops and mentally choosing the clothes for them, beginning with their shoes. This example is harder to follow for the characters in *Ghosts* because of the need to know something about the fashions of the period, but you could make a beginning by saying, 'If, say, Oswald were alive today what would he wear?' This approach is still limiting, because so many of the characters belong to their own age and no other. For instance, would there be many girls today in the same position as Regine?

So far, we have done no more than draw outlines. It is the task of the actor to fill in details and so bring the characters to life.

● Take each character in turn and test your knowledge of him or her by imagining a scene that Ibsen did not write but that could nevertheless be true within the given circumstances of the play. Here are a few ideas. You may wish to use others.

In some drinking den in the town Engstrand, half-seas over, is confiding to a crony his plans for opening a brothel, with his daughter as one of the inmates. He will express himself with his usual mixture of coarseness and hypocrisy. He hints that what he knows about the gentry will be enough to make sure that they don't get in his way.

Go back in time before the play begins. Mrs Alving confronts her husband with her knowledge of his relationship with Regine's mother.

Oswald is broken the news of his illness by his doctor.

Or go forward, after the play has ended. Manders gives an address on the sanctity of family life, having learned nothing at all.

Regine decides after all to join her father in his enterprise. She gives Mrs Alving notice and justifies her action.

5.5 Rehearsing the scene

When thinking about dividing an act into shorter sequences it sometimes helps to give each section a working title. For instance, the sequence between Mrs Alving and Manders mentioned in Unit 2 could be called 'The Books'. There is a later section that could be called 'Insurance'.

● Try to find similar titles for sequences within the acts.

Note that when the 'Insurance' sequence ends it is immediately followed by a reference to Engstrand's plans for his daughter. This is followed in its turn

5e   The Greenwich Theatre, 1974.

by Oswald's entrance with its strange effect upon Manders. The audience must be aware of this strangeness, even if Mrs Alving does not seem to be. The tension created here is not released until Manders's line 'the very spit and image of his father', and Mrs Alving's reaction, 'How can you say so! Oswald takes after me.' This is obviously a key exchange to which the actors and their director will have to give close attention. For the moment perhaps it is best regarded as a link with the next sequence, which is the strange story of Oswald while still a child being made by his father to smoke the very same pipe that he now holds in his hand.

Of course, this is skimming the surface to get an idea of the construction of the act, and passes by several places where very firm artistic decisions must be made. Before beginning to rehearse it is necessary to clear up any areas that are not clearly understood. Some lines appear to be rather obscure.

● Now return to the 'Insurance' sequence and examine it more closely. What are the steps in Manders's reasoning by which he persuades Mrs Alving not to insure the Orphanage? What is the connection between his reasoning and his inner feelings? How far is he aware that he is forcing Mrs Alving to take a dangerous decision?

● Play the scene through, paying attention to the way in which Mrs Alving is made to change her mind.

● Refer to Chapter 3.5. Then apply the Chekhov technique to Ibsen's play.

5.6   Realisation

● Consider the very last sequence of the play, the last ten speeches beginning at daybreak with the lamp still burning. Imagine how they would sound as a radio play. In some ways, this would be easier for the actors than to play the scene in a complete production on the stage.

● Work in pairs to rehearse the sequence. Then make recordings to compare and discuss with your colleagues.

No matter how well you have done it there will inevitably be something missing. The words alone are insufficient without the decor and the lighting.

● Note the contrasts between inside and outside the room, varying throughout the play.

● Go through the play and note all light and sound cues including the sound of rain. Do not spend too much time for the present discussing purely technical matters, concentrate on artistic decisions. What colours will you require on the backcloth of the mountain slopes and glacier? How will you light it?

(Refer to Unit 6 in other chapters.)

6
'Death of a Salesman' by Arthur Miller

First produced in 1949 in New York under the direction of Elia Kazan for the Group Theatre Company, who were well known for their adaptation of Stanislavsky's methods. The play received the Pulitzer Prize for drama. The part of Willy Loman was played in New York by Lee J. Cobb and in London by Paul Muni, later the same year. There was a marked difference in interpretation, Cobb being more extrovert than Muni in characterisation. The part has since been played on film by Fredric March and on the stage by a number of distinguished actors including Rod Steiger and Warren Mitchell. Hailed by some as a defence of the American ethos of prosperity through salesmanship the play has also been condemned as an attack upon American capitalism. It is published by Penguin (1949).

6.1 Barriers across the path

At first sight this play does not appear to present many difficulties to the contemporary British student or actor. A number of the ideas which were new in their time – the permanent set on the open stage, the touches of **expressionism** in a mainly realistic play and even the breaking of the unity of time – are no longer unfamiliar. Because of the amount of American entertainment available in Britain, British actors may be forgiven for presuming that *Death of a Salesman* would be easier to produce than a play by Shakespeare or a foreign masterpiece such as *Ghosts*. This feeling of familiarity may well be deceptive. The language seems easy to understand. It

Death of a Salesman *by Arthur Miller*

6a   Arthur Miller at the University of East Anglia, 1984.

is easy enough to make an approximate translation of an unfamiliar expression such as 'flunking math' and to guess at the process known as 'simonising' a car, but the British actor must learn not only to understand but also to speak American English. This is not simply a matter of putting on an American accent.

● Take five minutes to compile a list of recognisably different British accents and at the end of that time you will probably have at least a dozen if you take into account the effect of region and class inside a country tiny compared with the USA. How many different American accents do you suppose there are? And which is Willy Loman's? Would his sons speak differently from their father and from each other? How did Bernard speak as a schoolboy and what happened to his speech when he became a successful lawyer? (You can get records and tapes of most accents from the BBC and elsewhere.)

81

It is very desirable for actors working on this play to acquire the New York accent and to practise it until it becomes habitual. It sometimes helps the actors if they continue offstage conversations in their stage accent. In this way they tend to catch each other's intonations and the final effect is thus more acceptable because it is homogeneous.

If you find it difficult to acquire and maintain the accent then it is better to abandon the attempt and to concentrate on reproducing the speech rhythms in the text. After all, the sense and the feeling of the play should be paramount. It is not only good fun to listen to other people's accents and try to reproduce them but it teaches us a lot about speech techniques.

Although this play is realistic, the dialogue is by no means mundane. Miller has written that he considers the playwright to be a 'poet in the theatre' and classifies *Death of a Salesman* as a poetic tragedy. At first sight, this appears to be a strong claim, because we do not expect modern American English to bear comparison with the Greek of Aeschylus or the Renaissance language of Shakespeare, but Miller was not alone. Many other playwrights of his generation were deliberately experimenting with the use of poetic language in the theatre. Here is an extract from *Winterset* by Maxwell Anderson (Crown, 1939). The speaker, Esdras, is a Jewish–American scholar:

> I remember when I came to the end of all the Talmud
> said, and the commentaries,
> then I was fifty years old – and it was time to ask
> what I had learned. I asked this question
> and gave myself the answer. In all the Talmud
> there was nothing to find but the names of things,
> set down that we might call them by those names
> and walk without fear among things known.

In Clifford Odets's play *Golden Boy* (Crown, 1939) a young boxer, Joe, is speaking to his Italian-born father:

> Don't want to sit. Every birthday I ever had I sat around. Now'sa time for standing. Poppa, I have to tell you – I don't like myself, past, present and future. Do you know there are men who have wonderful things from life? Do you think they're better than me? Do you think I like this feeling of no possessions? Of learning about the world from Carp's encyclopaedia? Frank don't know what it means – he travels around, sees the world! [*Turning to* FRANK] You don't know what it means to sit around here and watch the months go ticking by! Do you think that's a life for a boy my age? Tomorrow's my birthday! I change my life!

To return to Miller, here is an extract from his later play *The Crucible* (Penguin, 1953), written in a reconstructed seventeenth-century English.

Death of a Salesman *by Arthur Miller*

The speaker, Danforth is one of the judges at a trial for witchcraft:

Mr Hale, believe me; for a man of such terrible learning you are most bewildered – I hope you will forgive me. I have been thirty-two year at the bar, sir, and I should be confounded were I called upon to defend these people. Let you consider, now – . . . . And I bid you all do likewise. In an ordinary crime, how does one defend the accused? One calls up witnesses to prove his innocence. But witchcraft is *ipso facto*, on its face and by its nature, an invisible crime, is it not? Therefore, who may possibly be witness to it? The witch and the victim. None other. Now we cannot hope the witch will accuse herself; granted? Therefore, we must rely upon her victims – and they do testify, the children certainly do testify. As for the witches, none will deny that we are most eager for all their confessions. Therefore, what is left for a lawyer to bring out? I think I have made my point. Have I not?

● Choose any of these extracts and read it aloud simply and sincerely and then discuss the function of the poet in the theatre.

The examples also remind us that American English is a synthesis of many other languages with the original colonial speech.

● *Death of a Salesman* contains many speeches to equal or surpass the examples given above. Find them and try speaking them.

The language conveys the feeling that lies at the heart of the play, but if we are going to try to act out that feeling then we must have accurate knowledge of the actual circumstances under which Willy Loman lived and worked and died.

This brings us to another barrier which may have been overlooked. This is the barrier of time. Miller is writing about America half a century ago. So we must ask and answer the question, 'What was it like to be a sixty-year-old salesman living in Brooklyn and travelling into New England in the 1940s?'

● Willy Loman must have been born in the 1880s. Imagine his British equivalent – a commercial traveller born at about the same time in London, say, and travelling to sell his firm's goods in East Anglia. Compare him with Willy Loman.

● Divide into groups and find out which historical events may have affected the lives of these men. Set up a series of meetings between them, perhaps at business conferences. What do they think of each other?

6b   Willy Loman, National Theatre, 1979.

● Now concentrate upon Willy's own lifetime. How would he have reacted
to the First World War and to the boom and depression which followed
it? Work out from the evidence in the play in what year he met and
married Linda and moved to Brooklyn. When were the boys born?
Where is Brooklyn? What sort of place might it have been for the Lomans
to wish to live there? What changes had taken place by the time the play
begins? Where might they have gone for a picnic?

6.2   Preparing for the task

The most difficult technical challenge in the play for the actors is to convey
the 'time-switch' changes that occur. This means that the actors playing Biff
and Happy have to switch from playing as men in their thirties to being
schoolboys in their teens, and back again. How many characters in the play
are called upon to do something like this?

At this point, it becomes necessary to break up the play into much smaller units than the two acts that Miller gives us.

● Work through the whole play (perhaps in two groups, one for each act) marking when the time-change scenes occur.

You will discover that there are at least two kinds of time-change. Sometimes time changes only for Willy himself, so that there is sometimes a sort of 'double image', as in the scene where he is playing cards with Charley and yet seeing and talking to Uncle Ben. When this occurs the other characters usually remain in their own present time and are upset by Willy's behaviour. There are also scenes in which everybody on the stage has been moved back in time. As in the 'polishing the car' sequence.

● Make detailed notes about these time changes and refer them to the historical time charts you have already made.

Now you can begin to study how the actors will show the passage of time in their physical movements. Avoid stereotype. Remember that a man of sixty, even if he is as exhausted as Willy Loman, is not a decrepit wreck. Shakespeare must take some of the blame for the perpetuation of this caricature of old age in Jaques' famous speech in *As You Like It* (see Chapter 2).

● Find the speech and try speaking it aloud. There would be nothing wrong in speaking it in an American accent because, after all, Shakespeare's English was the language of the first colonists in America.

● Now work out a sequence of pictures in movement for each of the characters. You will find that the peak of energy occurs at Shakespeare's fourth stage: 'The Soldier, jealous in honour, sudden and quick in quarrel'.

● Now put the words to the back of your mind and concentrate upon working out a *continuous* movement sequence from the baby lying on the floor at first, then sitting, kneeling, crawling, standing, walking, and then becoming the child going to school. Then go on through all the other stages until you become the old man gradually losing his faculties and declining into death.

At this point, if you are strongly interested in dance or mime, you could develop a solo performance or a dance for three characters – 'Person, Time and Death'. What sort of music would you use? To return to the use of this exercise in connection with the play, it will help you to substitute modern characterisations for Shakespeare's types. Who would you put between the child and the soldier? The student, perhaps. Again, the soldier might not be the best symbol for man at the height of his powers. What label could you use for him?

● Concentrate upon the stages most relevant to this play. What is the range of movement the actors will need to play in the 'time switches'?

Biff, Happy and Bernard switch from stage four, the active mature man, back to stage three, the student. Willy moves between stages four, five and six, and towards the end of the play, psychologically at least, he is approaching stage seven – the 'last scene of all'.

6.3 Exploring the background

Like millions of his fellow citizens then and now, Willy Loman firmly believed that his country is the finest on earth. He was typical not merely in his belief but in his readiness to express it. He and his wife and children were educated under a system in which there were regular and frequent ceremonies which involved swearing allegiance to the American flag.

Americans understand and feel such words as 'liberty', 'democracy' and 'freedom' rather differently from the British. Even as a salesman, Willy would have thought of his territory in a slightly different way from that of a British commercial traveller. He would tend to think of his journeys through the territory as in some way resembling those of the older pioneers, pushing back a frontier.

Americans frequently learn by heart the speeches of great American statesmen. Abraham Lincoln's address at Gettysburg at the time of the Civil War is one speech that Willy probably knew:

Four score and seven years ago, our fathers brought forth on this continent a new nation, conceived in liberty, and dedicated to the proposition that all men are created equal. Now we are engaged in a great civil war, testing whether that nation, or any nation so conceived and so dedicated, can long endure. We are met on a great battle-field of that war. We have come to dedicate a portion of that field as a final resting place for those who here gave their lives that that nation might live. It is altogether fitting and proper that we should do this.

But in a larger sense we can not dedicate, we can not consecrate, we can not hallow this ground. The brave men, living and dead, who struggled here, have consecrated it far above our poor power to add or detract. The world will little note, nor long remember, what we say here, but it can never forget what they did here. It is for us the living, rather to be dedicated here to the unfinished work which they who fought here have thus far so nobly advanced. It is rather for us to be here dedicated to the great task remaining before us – that from these honored dead we take increased devotion to that cause for which they gave the last full measure of devotion, that we here highly resolve that these dead shall not have died in vain, that this nation, under God, shall have a new birth of freedom, and that government of the people, by the people, for the people, shall not perish from the earth.

● How far could this speech be called 'poetic'? Compare it with the speeches in Unit 1 of this chapter. Try reading it aloud.

It would have been quite natural for Willy to have seen his profession as an extension of his patriotism. In his philosophy, the more goods he could sell the more money he would make to buy goods from other salesmen. Thus he would be expanding the economy and creating prosperity for his country.

During the 1930s employers used a number of devices to boost the morale of their salesmen. One of these was a weekly meeting usually conducted almost as if it was a religious gathering. Instead of hymns the salesmen joined in songs which set new words to well-known tunes, such as, 'Pack up your samples in your old black bag and sell, sell, sell!' There is no evidence in the play that Willy's firm ever used this method, but it is not unlikely that Howard Wagner might have considered it. Willy's own humble but sincere approach to salesmanship was ceasing to be typical at the time the play was written. Hence the controversy that immediately sprang up round it.

A completely irreverent approach occurs in *America Hurrah!* by Jean-Claude Van Itallie (Dramatists' Play Services Inc., 1966). The speaker is a gym instructor, running a class for sales personnel:

I took my last drag and strode manfully into the room. Okay, men, I said brightly. Let's see the basic step. *And* breathe it in and two and three and four. And breath it in and stick it out and three and four. Keep it nice. You want to radiate don't you? You want to radiate that charm and confidence they have in the movies, don't you, I told them. Now Ladies. *And* breathe it in and stick 'em out and step right out and four. *And* breathe it in and stick them out. Stick them out. That's what you got them for isn't it? I told them. And keep it nice, all of you. You're selling. Selling all the time. That's right, isn't it Miss? Right, I said. And stick it out and step right out and *smile*, I shouted. And breathe it in and stick it out, step right out and *smile*. Keep it nice. Keep it nice for the other fellow and you'll see how nice it can be for you. *Smile*. Only don't smile so big, I told them. You look like a bunch of creeps when you smile that big, I told them. Smile like you're holding something back, I said, something big, a secret, I said. That's the ticket. Now lets see it. *And* breathe it in and stick it out. Step on out and *nod*. Step on out and *shake*. And tuck in your butts, I yelled. Step on out and *smile*.

6.4 Characters and relationships

Every actor begins to study his character by reading his part and picking up the clues that the author has provided. Sooner or later, however, most actors find that they need to start asking questions about their character and discover that the author has given no specific answer.

It is much more rewarding for the actor when this happens, because he can feel that he is taking part in an act of creation when the author gives him a free hand. He can deepen his understanding of his character by improvising scenes that could have happened.

- Do not begin to experiment with this technique with scenes involving the major characters who are likely to be complex and even self-contradictory. Begin with important minor characters. For instance, consider the nameless Woman that Willy came to know. Work out a scene in which Willy meets her for the first time and they establish their relationship. Remember that the woman, according to Miller, is 'quite proper-looking'. She is not very young, but at the same time this is not a deeply serious love affair. Other scenes can be developed in the same way. First of all pick up the clues that the writer has provided and then base the scene upon them, adding any inventive detail you like, so long as it does not contradict the original information.

- Another possible scene could be built around Bernard as a boy, idolising Biff and trying to help him but being ignored by his hero. Charley makes his first appearance having been disturbed by Willy's unexpected return. He hears the car arrive very slowly. He discusses with somebody (perhaps Bernard) whether or not he should intrude. He fears that Willy is in serious trouble. He hears voices through the wall but cannot make out what is happening. What does he do?

- Invent similar scenes for characters such as Howard (taking on a new salesman to replace Willy), or between Stanley and the young waiter after Willy has caused a disturbance at the restaurant. In this way very small parts can be enriched in the hands of an imaginative actor to justify the famous saying of Stanislavsky: 'There are no small parts, only small actors' (see Chapter Three).

We have considered Willy as an American, as a salesman and as being typical in his generation, but so far, he does not appear to have the stature of a protagonist in a major **tragedy**. It is not that he is only a salesman, for we can accept that a salesman can be in some ways as noble as any king. Neither does it matter what he sells or even whether he is a good salesman.

What does he sell? Miller's answer to this was, 'He sells himself.' (Will the play work as well if we do not try to answer this question?) Is he a succesful salesman? (Examine the evidence in the play.) One theory of tragedy states that the hero of a tragedy should be a man otherwise noble but with a fatal flaw in his character. What is Willy's fatal flaw? Is it that, like King Lear, he has failed to know himself?

To turn to another question, do you think that it matters to the *performance* of the play whether Willy is clinically insane or not? Miller's original title for the play was *Inside his Head* and Willy certainly lives in a world created out of memory and imagination. A lot of people, especially elderly people, tend to do that. When we see such a person, perhaps staring into space and muttering, we may be amused or we may feel pity for them. Usually we say that such people are talking to themselves. This is not quite accurate. They are talking to a person whom they can see but we cannot. In this they resemble Willy Loman and also Macbeth in the banquet scene in Shakespeare's play:

[*The* GHOST OF BANQUO *enters, and sits in Macbeth's place*]
MACBETH: . . . Now good digestion wait on appetite,
   And health on both!
LENNOX: May't please your Highness sit. . . .
MACBETH: The table's full.
LENNOX: Here is a place reserv'd, sir.
MACBETH: Where?
LENNOX: Here, my good lord. What is't that moves your Highness?
MACBETH: Which of you have done this?
LORDS: What, my good lord?
MACBETH: Thou canst not say I did it; never shake
   Thy gory locks at me.
ROSSE: Gentlemen, rise, his Highness is not well.

Notice how Shakespeare does not over-dramatise the situation to start with. Macbeth begins quite calmly, simply puzzled because he is told that there is a place at the table when he can see that all the places are filled. He does not show strong emotion until one particular seat is pointed out to him and he recognises the person sitting there as the man he believes to be murdered by his command. With the Macbeth parallel in mind, prepare a walk-through reading of the following scene in Act One of *Death of a Salesman*:

[UNCLE BEN, *carrying a valise and an umbrella, enters the forestage from around the right corner of the house. . . .*]
WILLY: I'm getting awfully tired, Ben.
[BEN's *music is heard.* BEN *looks around at everything*].
CHARLEY: Good, keep playing; you'll sleep better. Did you call me Ben?
[BEN *looks at his watch.*]
WILLY: That's funny. For a second there you reminded me of my brother Ben.

6c Charley and Willy.

BEN: I only have a few minutes. [*He strolls, inspecting the place.* WILLY *and* CHARLEY *continue playing.*]

CHARLEY: You never heard from him again, heh? Since that time?

WILLY: Didn't Linda tell you? Couple of weeks ago we got a letter from his wife in Africa. He died.

CHARLEY: That so.

BEN: [*chuckling*] So this is Brooklyn, eh?

CHARLEY: Maybe you're in for some of his money.

WILLY: Naa, he had seven sons. There's just one opportunity I had with that man . . .

BEN: I must make a train, William. There are several properties I'm looking at in Alaska.

WILLY: Sure, sure! If I'd gone with him to Alaska that time, everything would've been totally different.

CHARLEY: Go on, you'd froze to death up there.

WILLY: What're you talking about?

BEN: Opportunity is tremendous in Alaska, William. Surprised you're not up there.

WILLY: Sure, tremendous.

CHARLEY: Heh?

WILLY: There was the only man I ever met who knew the answers.

CHARLEY: Who?

BEN: How are you all?

WILLY: [*taking a pot, smiling*] Fine, fine.

CHARLEY: Pretty sharp tonight.

BEN: Is Mother living with you?

WILLY: No, she died a long time ago.

CHARLEY: Who?

BEN: That's too bad. Fine specimen of a lady, Mother.

WILLY: [*to* CHARLEY] Heh?

BEN: I'd hoped to see the old girl.

CHARLEY: Who died?

BEN: Heard anything from Father, have you?

WILLY: [*unnerved*] What do you mean, who died?

CHARLEY: [*taking a pot*] What're you talkin' about?

BEN: [*looking at his watch*] William, it's half past eight!

WILLY: [*as though to dispel his confusion he angrily stops* CHARLEY'S *hand*] That's my build!

● Clear up the practical difficulties of the card game first. Find out the rules if you do not know them, or just make them up.

The basic questions to be answered by the actors playing this sequence are the same as those in the *Macbeth* scene. Who is speaking to whom? Who is visible to whom? How does Willy's state of mind change as the scene goes on? At the beginning of the scene Willy seems quite calm. He recognises Ben

6d Biff and Linda.

91

and is not disturbed by his presence, but what happens when Charley questions him?

While Willy is the protagonist of the play, Linda is the pivotal character; it would be a mistake to over-simplify her into a sentimentalised mother figure. She has one long speech in Act One, well worth speaking aloud, when she turns on Biff and Happy in order to reprimand them for their ingratitude. She has no mercy on their weaknesses, which she sees with more clarity than anger.

● Let the actress playing this part devise and perform two or three extra scenes to show Linda as the young woman meeting and being attracted by Willy; as the young wife and mother with the ribbon in her hair happy watching her children grow up and as the older woman when she first begins to realise that something terrible is happening to her husband.

She does not seem to have any existence outside her home and family. Surely she has neighbours, friends or relations? How far would it help the actress to improvise on those themes in order to make her a more rounded character? (See also Chapter Three.)

6.5 Rehearsing the scene

The audience are carefully prepared for the time switch into the long sequence in Act One set in the garden in the happy past of the Loman family. The director will have to take practical considerations into account. For instance, the time needed for Biff and Happy to prepare for their entrance must be covered by Willy's three solo speeches beginning while he is in the kitchen looking for the milk in the refrigerator. By the time Biff calls from off stage, the transition to the past should be complete.

● Read these speeches through and decide exactly when the scene change is made, particularly by means of the lighting.

Willy will need to rehearse the change in his manner of speaking, growing in strength and youthfulness. He has no opportunity for a change of make-up or costume. The change must be conveyed entirely by acting-skill. Strangely enough, when this is really well done in the theatre, nobody in the audience notices that it has been done at all!

The next sequence, from the entrance of the Loman brothers as young students, must move very quickly with no gaps left between cues.

● The two boys cavort around Willy like puppies but shadows of the future fall across the scene. Decide where these occur and how they will be indicated by changes in the pace of the dialogue.

92

Linda has more time to prepare for her entrance than the other characters in this scene. What changes will she have made in her make-up and costume? What changes will she have made in her speech and movement? Until her second entrance the audience have seen only the older Linda. This is a reversal of normal experience, so how does this affect the impact of her character?

● End the scene at the next time switch, which introduces the Woman. What sort of music accompanies her appearance? Should her laughter be amplified? How should the lighting change be used during this transition?

● Choose other scenes and work on them using a similar approach. (See Unit 5 of other chapters.)

6.6 Realisation

The setting offers little opportunities for individual expression by the scene-designer. It would be very unwise to attempt to make drastic alterations to the relationship of the rooms within the house, so the author's key scenic directions should be respected throughout.

As rehearsals proceed, design research could be carried on. Because of space limitations and the absence of walls in the house it will be found impracticable to furnish the house realistically. Willy and Linda would have had a lot of household gadgetry which would be faithfully reproduced for a film set but would be in the actors' way on the stage.

● Form groups to deal with the details. For instance, one group could research the interior furnishings for the house, another costumes, a third lighting and the fourth group could research a sound-script. Think in terms of **naturalism** and **expressionism**.

The noises from the apartment houses, or city sounds around the restaurant in the second act and the sound of Willy's car driving away at the end could provide a naturalistic element. There is also the expressionistic effect from the solo flute. The composing of this could be very interesting, bearing in mind that Miller asks for a tune which will *'tell of grass and trees and the horizon'*. There should be enough in this to keep the sound-script team busy for quite a while! Perhaps they could produce several versions for the rest of the company to choose from.

Lighting-designers will need to work through each of the small scenes in each act, bearing in mind time of day, season of year and the general mood of the scene, and prepare, not a technical lighting-plot (which can come later) but a broad specification of the lighting-requirements.

Again, which effects are *naturalist* and which *expressionist*? Which areas of the stage or set should be lit for each scene? With what colours and how brightly? Will there be any change of colour or intensity during the scene and will there be any areas deliberately left in darkness? If the scene is 'interior', will there need to be a lamp on the stage somewhere to be the apparent source of light? When the scene is 'exterior', how should the sky be lit – should this always be merely according to time and season or is it more important to use sky colour to indicate dominant mood? Can you use lighting to signal a time switch? How? In which scenes? Once the process of 'artistic' thinking is complete then the lighting-crew can go ahead and prepare the technical lighting-plan and lighting-plot.

In researching for wardrobe design, consider the differences in appearance that there must be between Linda, the Woman and Miss Forsythe. With this last character, designers could have fun by making her just a little bit *too*

6e   Uncle Ben and Willy Loman.

fashionable. But in what fashion? The American films of the period were usually meticulously researched for costume so old 'stills' are a mine of information. There is one character who does not need to be dressed completely realistically. This is Uncle Ben, who, after he has made his single 'real' appearance, becomes more and more a figment of Willy's imagination. The designer would be quite justified by dressing him in a slightly odd way for his later appearances.

7
'The Caucasian Chalk Circle' by Bertolt Brecht

Written between 1943 and 1945, while Brecht was in America, the play had its first professional production in East Berlin in 1954, directed by Brecht himself at the Teater am Schiffbauerdam with the Berliner Ensemble.

The first English production was directed by William Gaskill with the Royal Shakespeare Company at the Aldwych Theatre, London in 1962. Gaskill became known in this country as a leading director of Brecht's work. An interview with him published in *Encore* magazine in 1962 (see Booklist) is still an important document for English students.

References are to the edition translated by J. and T. Stern with W. H. Auden (Eyre Methuen, 1963).

7.1 Barriers across the path

Brecht is one of a very small number of major playwrights to have worked out a consistent theory of the function of theatre in society. This theory arose from his own experience in the German theatre between the wars. He probably thought about it in exile and returned to put it into practice in East Berlin in the 1950s. The basis of the theory is much easier to understand than some commentators seem to think. First of all, it is necessary to clear away misunderstandings that arise from the fact that Brecht was German and therefore inherited a tradition totally different from that operating in British theatre at the same time.

The Caucasian Chalk Circle *by Bertolt Brecht*

7a   Grusha, Wolsey Theatre, Ipswich.

If we compare mainstream British theatre from 1919 to the rise of Hitler with much German theatre over the same period we can tabulate the differences as follows:

BRITISH	GERMAN
(a) Domination by leading actors	Domination by directors
(b) Playwright important	Playwright not so important (his work could be rewritten)
(c) Naturalistic box sets	Expressionistic, symbolic settings, constructivist open stages
(d) Psychological acting (later influenced by Stanislavsky)	**Stylised** acting (influenced by Meyerhold and Piscator)
(e) Plot very important	**Theme** very important

BRITISH	GERMAN
(f) Theme absent or negligible	Plot negligible or illustrative only
(g) Main object to entertain	Main object to inform, to instruct, to persuade
(h) Very little attention to politics	Preoccupation with politics
(i) Where politics mentioned at all, generally right of centre	Politics usually left of centre
(j) Artistic policy sometimes inventive but conventional	Artistic policy consciously experimental
(k) Companies engaged by actor–managers for the run of the play	Ensemble companies, generally permanent, under one director
(l) Scene-setting usually naturalistic throughout a show	Use of interpolation of songs, back projection, direct narration, stylistic change, etc.

This is a simplification but it is worth bearing in mind that much that we take to be Brechtian is simply German. We must remember that the plays *seem* to be foreign because they *are* foreign. In this chapter, it is not intended to go very deeply into Brechtian theory, which is dealt with very ably elsewhere (see Booklist), but to concentrate on some aspects of his practical work.

It becomes obvious at a first reading that *The Caucasian Chalk Circle* bears many of the marks of a typical German epic. The first task of a company intending to produce it would be to divide into groups, each with a specific task concentrating on purely organisational problems. The first group should consider the cast list, which is very lengthy, and then work through the play to find out how far it is possible by doubling to reduce the number of actors required. (Gaskill had about twenty-four. Is this too many?) Six other groups could each take one of the numbered scenes and divide it into smaller sequences, noting the action of each sequence, and what scenery or stage furniture is necessary.

Then this information about continuity can be collated with the information discovered by the group that has been working on casting so that a schedule of exits and entrances can be worked out for the whole play so that each actor will know where he is supposed to be and what character he is playing at any given moment in the play. The interval is usually taken after Scene 4, a natural separation point between the story of Grusha and the story of Azdak.

Are there any clues to the chronology of the whole play? How much time elapses between the killing of the Governor and the trial in the chalk circle? Does the story of Azdak overlap in time with the story of Grusha?

All this business-like organisation calls for a high degree of company involvement and discipline. The ensemble approach may be made to a theme other than political. Helene Weigel, Brecht's wife suggested using Bible stories to a group of actors she once worked with in Finland. The great European legacy of Mystery plays from medieval Christian Europe have much in common with the works of Brecht. After all, the plays were written with didactic purpose and were performed by workers and peasants under the direction of intellectuals! The Bible is full of stories that can be treated in the same way as this story about a servant who saved a baby. In fact, one version of the trial inside the chalk circle can be found in the Bible with Solomon as the judge.

- Why not try such a story – the plagues of Egypt, for instance? Or the story of the Golden Calf. Play the improvisation in the way you are accustomed to. Do *not* try to be especially 'Brechtian', but try to give as sincere a performance as you can.

- Exploit the possibilities for reaction by a crowd of people to the same stimulus. This could be played as comedy at first – the reaction of the Egyptians to the plague of flies for instance. In the final plague it should be terrifying when, one by one, the firstborn sons collapse and die at the feet of their parents – Pharaoh's son last of all. Divide into small groups each taking one of the plagues.

7b   The Fat Prince, Ironshirts and The Singer.

● Do not permit a uniform reaction from the crowds as if they were a chorus-line in a musical. Note that Brecht never does this, even when his stage is packed with characters. Every one is an individual. If you choose the episode of the Golden Calf, in which the Israelites desert the God of their fathers for the new idol, make sure that each of them has his own reasons for doing so. When they return to the worship of their God, after being reprimanded by Moses, they doubtless had plausible excuses for their temporary lapse! Make up a few prayers: 'I'm sorry, Lord but it was like this . . .'

● When you have played one or both of these scenes discuss the ways in which your improvisations were similar to the crowd scenes in the play and in what way they may have differed.

A Brechtian actor must first of all be a competent actor, capable of effective speech and movement and preferably able to sing, dance and use at least one of the specialist theatre techniques, such as tumbling or conjuring. He should be capable of impersonating recognisable characters based upon observation, perhaps two or three or even more during one play. He must be able to interact with his fellow actors and above all he must be aware of the **theme** with which the play is concerned.

One of his special attributes is his ability to change roles rapidly and completely.

● To practise this skill, set up a chair or some other marker in the middle of the acting-area. Enter from one side as one character, for example, a drunken soldier. When you reach the chair, pause, take a deep breath and then continue your journey as a monk meditating upon the scriptures.

Every actor should be a constant observer if he is to avoid melodrama or stereotypes.

● Make a point of regular observation of people in public places. Make notes of what you see. When you have found a particularly interesting scene, narrate it exactly as it occurred using the words actually used and reproducing the tone of voice of the speaker. Add nothing except necessary brief descriptions of the people concerned and omit nothing essential.

● Take it in turn to relate such stories to your group. Do not regard this as a competition in any way.

Some people find that they cannot *tell* without *demonstrating*. That is to say that they find that they need to help the narration with gesture or to half-impersonate the person they are describing. This is not 'breaking the rules' if this is your natural way of giving an account of something you have seen, but beware of the actor's tendency to embroider the scene to make it effective. You should be concerned with telling the objective truth as you saw it and nothing else.

● When you have all told your stories, repeat the character-changing exercise that you did earlier, but instead of using the characters you invented for that occasion use two of the real characters that you have observed and described.

These exercises will make it easier for you to read and discuss Brecht's famous article *The Street Scene* which is reprinted in several books (see Booklist).

Here is what Brecht himself had to say on the matter in one of his poems:

Showing has to be Shown

Show that you are showing! Among all the varied attitudes
Which you show when showing how men play their parts
The attitude of showing must never be forgotten.
All attitudes must be based on the attitude of showing
This is how to practise: before you show the way
A man betrays someone, or is seized by jealousy
Or concludes a deal, first look
At the audience, as if you wished to say:
'Now take note, this man is now betraying someone and this is how he does it,
This is what he is like when jealousy seizes him, and this
Is how he deals when dealing.' In this way
Your showing will keep the attitude of showing
Of putting forward what has been made ready, of finishing off
Of continually going further. So show
That what you show is something you show every night, have often shown before
And your playing will resemble a weaver's weaving, the work of a
Craftsman. And all that goes with showing
Like your continual concern to
Make watching simpler, always to ensure the best
View of every episode – that too you should make visible. Then
All this betraying and dealing and
Being seized by jealousy will be as it were
Imbued with something of the quality of a
Daily operation, for instance of eating, saying Good Morning and
Doing one's work. (For you are working, aren't you?) And behind your
Stage parts you yourselves must still be visible, as those who
Are playing them.

If you prepare the poem for reading or speaking aloud you will not only be giving yourself valuable technical practice but you will begin to see the relationship between Brecht and his actors. In some ways, the poem may remind you of the famous lines by Shakespeare that we know as 'Hamlet's advice to the players' (see Chapter One). Notice how Brecht calls attention to the power of habit. As we shall see later in this chapter, half of what passes for characterisation is no more than the depiction of habitual movement. Also, Brecht greatly admired craftsmen of all kinds. To say that an actor's work resembles 'a weaver's weaving' was, for him, a very high compliment. Finally, in one of the lines there is the hint of directorial authority – 'For you are working, aren't you?' When you speak the poem, pay particular attention to the subtlety of this parenthetical sentence.

Much of the difficulty that British actors have with playing Brechtian style arises from the way they were trained, mainly by teachers who were influenced by Stanislavsky (see Chapter Three). This is also true for anybody whose interest in drama was first aroused by taking part in open-ended improvisation at school. Brechtian improvisation is *never* open-ended. It serves a totally different purpose from improvisation in educational drama and in theatres in which the Stanislavsky method is used. In these places improvisation is used to explore an emotional situation, whether in real life or in a piece of scripted drama.

This may be interesting and exciting because it provides an opportunity for those taking part to learn more about themselves and more about the art of theatre. The original situation is merely a starting-point which can be amended or changed, but with Brecht the story line does not change. The actor uses improvisation as a method of 'checking against reality'. To get into Brechtian habits of improvisation try the following exercises:

● First, one of the actors relates something that he saw happen as in the exercise above. Next, the group plays out the scene trying to make it exactly as he described it. Then, in consultation with the original narrator and any other available witnesses they discuss whether or not the improvisation was truthfully performed. This means that the actors have to be very much aware of what they are attempting. And this is a beginning of the understanding of the **'A effect'**.

7.2 Preparing for the task

This play is set in the past before the invention of gunpowder and, just as the play itself is in two parts, an outer or containing play and an inner play, which points the moral, so the actors could think of themselves as playing roles within roles.

As we have seen, Brecht expects us to be aware of the actor all the time he is in front of us 'showing' his character. In this play the character he shows *first* is a peasant. This may be particularly helpful to the British actor, who may have difficulty in presenting a peasant character. Over much of the world, the tradition of peasantry remains, but in England it died centuries ago. Whether playing Grusha or the Governor's Wife, it would be necessary to lay the foundation of peasant first.

For people who live a reasonably comfortable and sheltered life, the first step is to experience discomfort, hard work and bad weather. Joan Littlewood, the founder and first director of the Theatre Workshop Company which took over the Theatre Royal, Stratford, London, shared many of Brecht's political and artistic theories. When preparing a play about prison life she made her actors follow prison routines for hours on end, being locked into small rooms, forbidden to talk, fed on prison food, and exercised by walking in circles on the theatre roof. This may seem extreme, and was certainly painful for the actors, but at least it gave them something of an experiential reference point. If you were to apply this technique to this play then you would have to live as medieval peasants for a time.

● Since you cannot travel in time back to the Middle Ages, undertake the following activities in actuality rather than in the imagination, and carry them on just long enough to experience real discomfort. Without using power tools or any well-sharpened instruments, cut or drill hard, tough wood; dig hard, stony or soggy soil; sew heavy cloth by hand with coarse thread; wash heavy clothes in an old-fashioned copper; lift and carry heavy weights. Try to think of other similar tasks that might have been carried out habitually by peasants. If you wish further to deepen your experience of peasant life, try performing the tasks under extreme conditions, such as being very cold, very wet and very hungry.

● Do not, of course, risk your health in pursuit of artistic truth, but if you carry these tasks out you may well begin to discover something about the physical nature of the peasant. Immediately you come to the end of a particular task, notice which muscles in the body are experiencing strain, then consider what the effect would be on your posture and movement if such strain was habitual. Then look at some paintings of peasants, the work of the Breughels, for instance, or photographs of peasants today in China and elsewhere.

The following sequence of games is intended to show how to lead from general activities to those more specific to the play.

● Try the well-known children's pushing-game called *The Raft of Medusa*, which involves all the players being crowded together within the confines of a marked-out square. The object of the game is to become the sole survivor by pushing everybody else off the raft into the sea. People who have been pushed off may become 'sharks' and have the right to grab at any limb which projects over the edges of the raft. (There are many variations of this according to where the actors may first have learnt it.) The game can be used to provide a starting-point for activity intended to fill the whole stage.

● When the game is going really well and is getting nice and rough, the director may call out, 'Freeze!' Everybody should then stop dead in whatever position they find themselves. The director may then give the instruction, 'Take it from where you are now. You are in a medieval battle.' Or the actors could be in a street riot during a revolution, or they could be victims of a hurricane, or in whatever situation is going to be required.

There are several occasions in this play where this technique could be applied. The *Raft of Medusa* game can also be used to introduce a major theme from the play by appointing the winning survivors to become the dominant characters in the next game, the 'Nobs' and all the others 'Peasants'.

7c Azdak.

● Nobs have the right to boss peasants about and give them orders. Peasants must obey or get hit by the nobs with harmless weapons such as balloons or rolled-up newspapers. Peasants may not hit back or they become 'executed' and are out of the game. On the other hand, they may clown about behind a Nob's back, mocking him. If detected, they get hit.

● The selection of the Nobs need not always depend upon having won a previous game. Sometimes the director may select the Nobs according to a whimsical rule of his own, such as 'Everybody with blue eyes is a Nob' or 'Anybody wearing green is a Peasant'. This method is just as sociologically true as any other.

● After the game has been played for some time, allow Nobs and Peasants to change roles. Discuss whether a Nob will treat his Peasants more kindly if he knows he is likely to become one himself, or whether a Peasant once promoted will necessarily become a kindly Nob, in the game or in real life.

Between the games and the first run-through of some of the scenes there should be a period of rest in which the actors may begin to refine their ideas about the peasant role and how they can use it as the core of an individual character.

● Consider how the following stage direction could be brought to life:

> BEGGARS *and* PETITIONERS *stream from a palace gateway, holding up thin children, crutches, and petitions. They are followed by two* IRONSHIRTS *and then by the* GOVERNOR'S *family, elaborately dressed.*
> THE BEGGARS AND PETITIONERS: Mercy, Your Grace, the taxes are beyond our means . . . I lost my leg in the Persian War, where can I get . . . My brother is innocent, Your Grace, a misunderstanding . . . My child is starving in my arms . . . We plead for our son's discharge from the army, our one remaining son . . . Please, Your Grace, the water inspector is corrupt.
> *A* SERVANT *collects the petitions, another distributes coins from a purse.* SOLDIERS *push back the crowd, lashing at it with thick leather whips.*

Of course, we have been oversimplifying. Even the mythical world of this play has a much more subtle class structure than we have so far postulated. As you work through the play you will notice that there are times when a Nob gets treated as badly as any Peasant and that some Peasants seize upon chances to behave like Nobs. Some of this behaviour is more concerned with *status* than with rank and will be dealt with in the following chapter. The following thematic improvisation can now be played out. It shows that, according to Brecht, the structure of society remains unaltered although the fortunes of individuals may change.

● Nobs are selected as before by chance or by winning a previous game.

● Nobs proceed, as before, to order the rest of the company as Peasants to do various jobs and beat them when the Peasants do not please them.

● Nobs get tired and bored with this, so they select strong reliable Peasants to supervise the work of the rest.

● These promoted Peasants are given the weapons of punishment to use on the rest. The Nobs at first enjoy watching the promoted Peasants (whom they now call Ironshirts) keeping the others in order.

● What happens when there is a quarrel among the Nobs?

● Work this out as an improvisation and compare your plot line with the first half of the play.

7.3 Exploring the background

● Put the 'containing play' into a British context by trying one of the following improvisations.

● Take a theme involving a public dispute over the use of land. For instance: plans for a much needed by-pass may offend conservationists or farmers. Base your dramatisation of a public inquiry on facts as far as possible. Divide into three groups: two large ones, respectively 'pro' and 'anti', and one small one, the court. You may develop interesting characters but you must stick to the agreed facts.

● Imagine an isolated house close to the frontier of a continental country. War came, the house was damaged and the owners fled. The war moved on and refugees came and occupied the house. They repaired it and tended the garden. Peace came. The owners returned. Dramatise the confrontation.

● Imagine a situation in which a child could be abandoned and rescued as Michael is in the play. Develop the plot differently in modern circumstances. Imagine that Michael whilst still quite young becomes rich and famous perhaps as a successful pop-star. Now imagine that his real mother suddenly turns up. How does he react?

● Having carried out all the preceding activities discuss what you now think about the idea of ownership, as it applies to land, to property and to people.

7.4 Characters and relationships

Once more, we are reminded of the differences between Brecht and Chekhov as writers and between Brecht and Stanislavsky as directors. If an actor is preparing to appear in a play by Chekhov such as *The Seagull* (see Chapter Three), he is likely to begin to study the play from the point of view of his character. He must learn the personal history of his character and understand his psychology – his hopes, fears, and desires. From this knowledge he can formulate *objectives* for the character. Until he has done this he is unable to bring the character to life.

The theory behind this approach presumes that most people are in fact emotionally motivated. Brechtian theory suggests that a lot of our actions are more likely to arise from habit or from economic motives. Gaskill, in the interview mentioned in the introduction to this chapter, pointed out that Shakespeare's murderers are not necessarily evil sadists but can be portrayed as professionals who happen to get their living by murder. Since murder was a recognised profession in Shakespeare's time, he would have expected assassins to have certain habitual ways of going on but no special delight in being evil.

Again, since Brechtian theatre is a didactic theatre it follows that the ideas it discusses are going to be more important than any development of character.

● Form groups according to status or occupation within the play, such as 'peasant', 'noble', 'Ironshirt'. First of all, decide what you have in common that can be immediately perceived as the mark of your group. For instance, the peasants should agree upon a common manner of speech. Other similarities must be established. This does not imply that every member of each group must always look and sound identical with his fellows, but habits of speech, gesture, posture, stance and movement all distinguish the noble from the peasant and both from the soldiers. Perhaps there is a difference between the ordinary soldier and the Ironshirts similar to that between members of training units in Britain and a crack regiment such as the Paratroopers.

Once the group-role has been established and each actor has become familiar with it, the next step is to introduce the individual differences that bring the character to life. This should never be done by introducing irrelevant mannerisms simply to make a character stand out in a crowd. Some characters need to be developed not by the process of 'addition' of characteristics, but rather with a 'subtraction' or contradiction of characteristics. An example of this is Georgi Abashvili, the Governor. He is a nobleman but not as complete a nobleman as the Fat Prince. The Governor's time seems to be spent in giving banquets and talking to architects about his dream palaces. In other words he is a failure as a nobleman, because he is neglecting the war which is threatening his province. It does not matter whether he is a patron of the arts or not. As an aristocrat he is a failure and therefore he is destroyed, as Brecht shows us, by the society in which he lives.

● Look out for changes in group behaviour. Notice how the servants, for instance, become much more self-assured towards the end of Scene 2 when the nobles have fled, and also how the Ironshirts at the beginning of Scene 5 behave like noblemen even towards the Fat Prince.

● Play through the sequence in the middle of Scene 3 when Grusha tries to join the ladies at the inn. Notice the moment at which the demeanour of the ladies changes and find reasons for this. Change the character of the Innkeeper. Make him younger and less dignified, but still an innkeeper. Does the *point* of the scene change much?

The two central characters, Grusha and Azdak cannot be considered in isolation from each other. It would help the actors to have a discussion with the entire company about the similarities and differences between the two roles. We could start from the assumption that Grusha who combines goodness and innocence with a certain ignorance of the ways of the world could never have saved Michael but for Azdak's cunning and worldly wisdom. Does this mean that these are merely two sides of a single symbolic character? Note that neither of these characters seems to have been written as a part for a romantic leading player. Brecht made a point of choosing his actors for being ordinary-looking, unhandsome and undistinguished.

● Finally, consider the implications for what we have been saying about Brechtian characterisation of the following extract from one of Azdak's speeches. He is talking to the Grand Duke, now a fugitive and pretending to be a beggar. He has asked Azdak to help him.

So old and yet so cowardly! Finish your cheese, but eat it like a poor man, or else they'll still catch you. Do I even have to tell you how a poor man behaves? . . . Put your elbows on the table, and now surround the plate with your arms as though you expected the cheese to be snatched from you at any moment. What right have you to be safe? Now hold the knife as if it were a small sickle; and don't look so greedily at your cheese, look at it mournfully – because it's already disappearing – like all good things.

7.5 Rehearsing the scene

● First, concentrate upon a scene that does not call for a large crowd of people. A good example begins in Scene 3 where Grusha, having left Michael with the peasants is retracing her steps in the hope of joining Simon and encounters the two Ironshirts (p. 35 in the Eyre Methuen text). End the scene at the moment when, triumphant but delirious she has escaped across the bridge.

● Decide how the entire sequence will fit into the acting-area at your disposal and in particular how you would solve the problem of setting the Rotten Bridge. Where will the peasant's house be? Solve any other practical problems before you begin a walkthrough with books in hand.

● Experiment with speaking the lines in different ways and look back in the play to see if any of the characters have appeared before. If so, their speech and general behaviour must be consistent with their last appearance. For new characters you will have a chance to invent in Brechtian terms. (Do you agree that the undressing of Michael is the key action in this scene and not as we might expect the actual escape across the bridge?)

7d   The Wedding-Funeral party, with 'invisible' wall.

- To approach a full-scale crowd scene such as the funeral–wedding in Scene 4 begin with the *Raft of Medusa* game (see Unit 2). When your director shouts 'Freeze!', imagine that you are eating and drinking in a ridiculously overcrowded small room. Some guests are under the table, others are sitting in each other's laps. Plates of food and mugs of drink are being passed to people who need them. Empty plates and mugs are being passed back for replenishment, and so on. Everybody is very polite and very happy and conversing at the tops of their voices.

- Now work out in what order this party will break up when the bridegroom 'rises from the dead' and drives them out. Some go out of the doors, others out of the windows.

- Then compile an action plot beginning at the stage direction at the top of p. 49 ('*a space divided by a partition . . .*') and ending on p. 55 at the stage direction '*The guests stampede from the house.*' Without considering dialogue except for providing the cues, work through all the necessary action so that one event seems to rise naturally out of the other. Solve the problem of keeping the main plot line perfectly clear in spite of the comic detail going on all round it.

7e Azdak contesting to become a judge.

7.6 Realisation

THE EXPERT: How long will the story take, Arkadi? I have to get back to
   Tiflis tonight.
THE SINGER: It is actually two stories. A few hours.
THE EXPERT: [*very confidentially*] Couldn't you make it shorter?
THE SINGER: No.

The play is fairly long but very difficult to cut. If you refer to the action
schedules that you have compiled you will see that there is a danger of losing
time at every scene change, especially in stage waits if an actor is not ready
with a new characterisation.

Also, clothing must be designed so that it can be rapidly changed and
make-up kept simple for the same reason. Masks have practical uses. You
could develop the idea of using masks for Nobs with some character
variations, especially for the Governor's wife. How would you design them?
What materials would you use?

There are one or two major pieces of scenery which need to be carefully
designed and properly placed. What are they? Major scenic effects will come
from the lighting, especially on the back wall or cyclorama.

What do you think should be done about music? Do you need to research
into the music of medieval China? Or could you use modern melodies and
instrumentation? Need the narrator be a singer?

8
'The Sea' by Edward Bond

First produced at the Royal Court Theatre, London, and directed by William Gaskill on 22 May 1973 with a cast including Coral Browne, Ian Holm and Alan Webb. Bond had been a member of the Writers' Group at the theatre in the 1950s. *The Pope's Wedding* (1965) was his first play to get a full production and began a series which ended with *The Sea.* The plays are linked by differing treatments of allied social themes.

References are to the Eyre Methuen edition (1975) with notes by the author, and to *Edward Bond: A Companion to the Plays*, by Malcolm Hay and Philip Roberts (TQ Publications, 1978).

8.1 Barriers across the path

Bond's reputation as a 'difficult' playwright began in 1966 when his second play, *Saved*, because a *cause célèbre* because of a scene in which two young men stoned a baby to death in its pram. The Lord Chamberlain ordered cuts to be made in the play. Bond refused. Legal action was then taken against him and the theatre. Public discussion about the case intensified the existing dissatisfaction with the Lord Chamberlain's powers of theatre censorship. These were eventually abolished in 1968.

Bond stands apart from every other playwright of his generation. He has always been involved in controversy, not always of his own making. In the early days it was supposed by some of the critics that because he depicted scenes of violence he was advocating violence or using it purely for its own sake. In fact, he holds very strong pacifist views, which are part of a general personal philosophy which leads him to be highly critical of all present systems of government.

He thinks of the writing of plays as a kind of public service to initiate discussion of important political matters. Therefore, he is sometimes impatient of people who wish to discuss his plays within a limited context of 'art'. For him, art and politics are so strongly bound up with each other that they cannot be discussed separately. For Bond, much artistic criticism is pointless. He once wrote that a man who is shouting 'Fire!' does not wish to be congratulated on how well he shouts. He simply wants somebody to help him to put out the fire.

On the other hand, he is always willing to help directors and actors working on his plays by providing copious programme notes and explanatory material to go into published versions. He has done so for this play in the Eyre Methuen edition. The notes are worth reading and rereading, but for present purposes we can concentrate on two particular sentences.

The first is: 'Evolution is the record of failure at the same time as it's the record of success'. This can be taken as a general philosophical statement.

The second, particular to this play, is: 'The sea also stands for hope'. This may help to explain why this play is deliberately unfinished. In the theatre it ends with Willy, the character whom we might possibly describe as the hero, talking to Evens, the man who lives alone in a hut on the beach.

WILLY: Should I stay in the town? Work hard. Make money. Become mayor.

EVENS: No. Go away. You won't find any more answers here. Go away and find them. Don't give up hope. That's always silly. The truth's waiting for you, it's very patient, and you'll find it. Remember, I've told you these things so that you won't despair. But you must still change the world.

ROSE *comes on.*

ROSE: I followed you. The packing's finished. We mustn't miss our train. I saw you talking. What were you saying?

WILLY: I came to say goodbye, and I'm glad you –

The hero and the heroine having met in shared suffering and perhaps found love for each other are not going off to be happy ever after. They are at a new beginning. The two most sane and sensible people in the play survive to live on in another place. It is this fact that makes this play a **comedy**, and not a **tragedy.**

One cause of confusion is the absence of any conventional exposition. The play begins at a 'high point' with a stage direction arousing contradictory emotions in the reader.

Beach. Empty stage. Darkness and thunder. Wind roars, whines, crashes and screams over the water. Masses of water swell up, rattle and churn, and crash back into the sea. Gravel and sand grind slowly. The earth trembles.

8a Willy and Rose.

The reader sitting quietly at home may be grateful for the superb mental picture created, but a director contemplating production might have his pleasure spoilt by wondering how on earth he could create such an effect upon his stage. (It can be done, without using extraordinary resources. Back projection may help, but the scene depends upon precise acting.)

● Prepare to give a performance of the scene, not necessarily in full as written, but of its *essence*. Before you can do this you must be aware of the four components of the scene – the three men and the sea. Read the author's note. Do not expect to be able to understand everything that he writes. Try to arrive at a working hypothesis on your own terms, of his idea of the sea as being both negative and positive, destructive and yet providing hope. (It may help to stimulate your imagination for this and other exercises to have a tape of different sea sounds, including a terrific storm, ready to play as a background to the action.)

● Now consider not the *characters* of each of the three men, but what they *do*.

If this were being treated according to the doctrines of Stanislavsky you might have compiled a complete biography for Willy. You would need to know more about Colin, the man who was in the boat when it capsized. You would also have thought out the reasons for the voyage. If you were playing

Hatch you would have known the reasons for his insanity as well as the form it takes. Similarly you would be aware, if you were playing the part, that, while Evens is drunk on this occasion, he is not an alcoholic, but capable of wisdom. But this is not a **naturalistic** play by Chekhov. It is a **symbolic** play by Bond.

All you need to try to convey to the audience has been written in the dialogue and stage directions.

> Willy is in the water trying to find where his friend is and at the same time calling for help.

> Evens is on the beach, drunk and singing. He pays no attention to Willy.

> Hatch approaches Evens and speaks to him as if he thinks Evens is concerned with some crime or other.

> Evens goes off. Willy comes out of the water into the beam of Hatch's torch. He appeals for help but Hatch drives him back into the sea.

> Hatch hears the guns and seems to think that they are firing at Willy. This pleases Hatch who regards Willy as an enemy.

> Willy runs through the sea still shouting for Colin but no longer expecting help.

- Using the foregoing as a series of stage directions and improvising only such dialogue as is absolutely necessary, play the scene through against the background of the noise of the sea.

- Do not aim for naturalism; that is to say, do not try to make it 'seem real'. Just try to get the feeling of the symbolic content.

- When you have played this through perhaps more than once in different versions, discuss its function in the play. Is it merely an opening scene? Or is it more of a prologue? Does it serve a function similar to that of the 'dumbshow' in Elizabethan plays? Does it remind you of the opening of *Macbeth* or any other Shakespeare play?

- Do not fall into the trap of regarding the play as a series of riddles, to which there will be a series of simple answers. You are not likely to find many answers but with luck you will uncover some very interesting questions.

The use of **symbolism** in plays may be unfamiliar today, but it is not necessarily difficult to understand. Most symbolic acts are basically simple.

They occur as the climax of most important ceremonies. Their function is to remind the people concerned of the importance of what they are doing. In the wedding-ceremony the symbolic dramatic action is the placing of the ring on the bride's finger, in a coronation the placing of the crown upon the head of the new king.

● Think of other, similar examples and act them out. Notice how often such acts include the use of 'stage properties' such as the ring and the crown. Are the curtains in this play symbolic properties?

This play has many scenes which are very funny in themselves. If you examine them closely you will notice that the humour arises mainly from the behaviour of two people in the play. Mr Hatch is obviously mad. So is Mrs Rafi, but less obviously so at first.

Hatch's obsession with invaders from space seems very unlikely for 1907, but look up dates of publication of early science fiction. Could Hatch have read H. G. Wells? The important thing about Hatch's obsession is that it is an illusion based upon truth in the sense that it is the persecution mania of a man who is actually being persecuted.

The insanity of Mrs Rafi is more dangerous because a number of people around her seem to accept her delusions of grandeur without question. In the *Companion to the Plays* Bond compares *The Sea* with his first play, *The Pope's Wedding*.

8b   Hollarcutt, Hatch, Carter and Thompson.

116

The Sea *by Edward Bond*

The Sea is about the problems that all my other plays are concerned with. It's a sort of counterpart – a comedy as opposed to a tragedy – of my first play *The Pope's Wedding*. Both plays are about the pursuit of illusions – of false solutions to political and personal problems. (The two are far more closely connected than most people like to admit.) In *The Pope's Wedding* there is no escape for the protagonists. But *The Sea* is a comedy, and so there is – for some of them. Like the young couple in *The Tempest*, Willy and Rose have to create their own personal maturity. The ideal figure is drowned and lost . . . .

It may be helpful to consider Bond in comparison with other playwrights whose work has been considered in this book. He resembles both Ibsen and Brecht in his preoccupation with moral and political questions, but he is nearer to Brecht than to Ibsen. It may be significant that much of his work has been directed by William Gaskill, who is well known in Britain as a producer of Brecht, but nobody would mistake a single page of Bond for a page of Brecht.

Unlike Chekhov, Bond does not create detailed characters with complete biographies and psychologies. Unlike Miller, Bond does not seek to build upon literary traditions of drama. This may be because he learned his craft within an experimental theatre, using improvisatory methods. (See Unit 2, below.) Unlike Wilde, he aims to do more than simply entertain, but if *The Sea* does not work as entertainment then its symbolism will not work either.

8.2 Preparing for the task

The following series of exercises is not necessarily specific for working on the plays of Bond or indeed any particular kind of play. They were devised as a rapid means of turning a group of assorted individuals into a company willing and able to cooperate physically and artistically. The more demanding the play, the greater the need for co-operation.

The first exercise is called *A Chair is a Chair is Not a Chair*.

● The company, having met for the first time, is permitted by the director to remain seated for a very brief while. He then suggests that everybody stand up and examine the chair on which he has been sitting. Are all the chairs the same? What are they made of? How far are they really fit for their purpose? Are any of them showing signs of age or weakness?

● The next stage is for each actor to consider the chair as if it were anything but a chair. For instance, it can be used *as if* (these are magic words – see Chapter Three) it were a lawnmower, then perhaps an old hand-driven lawnmower being pushed across a stony patch of grass or as if it were a pram, then perhaps a pram containing a noisy and nasty infant. Once we begin to get really inventive the chair can be used as if it were a pram containing a noisy and nasty infant that somebody is trying to kidnap. And so on, until everybody has turned their chair into something interesting, exciting, ridiculous or possibly even beautiful.

● The lawnmowers, prams, and so on, can now be allowed to revert to becoming chairs while the next stage is explained. The company now forms itself into pairs or threes and with the *absolute minimum of discussion* puts the two or three chairs together with the two or three bodies to make something new – something that can be a large and a small dog sharing a kennel, or mermaids swimming towards a lighthouse or anything else that might occur.

● The game then continues with slightly larger groups, say about six or seven, with their chairs and also any other oddments the director may have left lying about for the purpose. (These could include pieces of cloth, garden canes, string, etc.) As before, there should be a minimum of discussion; communication should be through action inviting co-operation until something emerges. After an agreed limited time, the products are shown by each group to the others, perhaps with a title, perhaps as a guessing-game. Then the arrangement is left where it stands and each group moves round and takes possession of somebody else's *objet d'art* and uses that as a given starting-point for a new act of creation.

Students should be warned not to be too solemn and not to aim to create recognisable stage-settings. There are two golden rules for success in this kind of work.

● *Do not discuss until you have created something that is worth discussing.* In other words do not solemnly sit down on the chairs (which are the basic raw material) and talk about what might possibly be done. Possibilities are infinite and if you are going to discuss them all you will never begin to do anything. On the other hand, as soon as anybody has an idea he should begin to *act* it in such a way that at least one of his colleagues is being invited to join in. For instance, if you think it might be a good idea to begin by inverting a table and using it as a raft on a stormy sea, do not *suggest* or even *tell* your colleagues what you are about to do, just be bold and 'swim' towards your raft, climb exhausted aboard, cling on for dear life and hail anybody who needs your help.

● *Remember the context in which the improvisation takes place*, otherwise improvisation becomes self-indulgence. Our context is theatrical, concerned directly with this particular play and author.

The battle, central to the play, between Mrs Rafi and Hatch is expressed through the status relationship between them. At this point we need to refer to the work of a director and teacher, Keith Johnstone, who worked with Edward Bond when the writer was 'learning the business' at the Royal Court Theatre. The following extract is from his book *Impro*.

> I ask a group to mill about and say 'hallo' to each other. They feel very awkward, because the situation isn't *real*. . . . I then get some of the group to hold all eye contacts for a couple of seconds, while the others try to make and then break eye contacts and then immediately glance back for a moment. The group suddenly looks more like a 'real' group, in that some people become dominant, and others submissive. Those who hold eye contacts report that they feel powerful – and actually look powerful. Those who break eye contact and glance back 'feel' feeble, and look it. The students *like* doing this, and are interested, and puzzled by the strength of the sensations. I might then begin to insert a tentative 'er' at the beginning of each of my sentences, and ask the group if they detect any change in me. They say that I look 'helpless' and 'weak' but they can't, interestingly enough, say what I'm doing that's different. . . . Then I move the 'er' into the middle of sentences, and they say that they perceive me as becoming a little stronger. If I make the 'er' longer, and move it back to the beginning of sentences, then they say I look more important, more confident. When I explain what I am doing, and let them experiment, they're amazed at the different feelings the length and displacement of the 'ers' give them. . . . The short 'er' is an invitation for people to interrupt you; the long 'er' says 'Don't interrupt me, even though I haven't thought what to say yet'.

Another trick Johnstone taught his students was how to gain authority simply by keeping the head still when speaking.

> You can talk and waggle your head about if you play the gravedigger, but not if you play Hamlet. . . . My belief (at this moment) is that people have a preferred status; that they like to be low, or high, and that they try to manoeuvre themselves into the preferred positions. A person who plays high status is saying 'Don't come near me, I bite.' Someone who plays low status is saying, 'Don't bite me, I'm not worth the trouble.' In either case the status played is a defence, and it'll usually work.

● Check the truth of Johnstone's statements from your own observations.

● Try some of the activities and then apply your findings to the play. Which characters play 'high status' and which 'play low'?

8.3 Exploring the background

Bond frequently describes his work as the 'theatre of reason'. For Bond, the causes of irrationality, of insanity, lie within society. If a society is itself mad, then the people within it will be driven mad. He has written his own version of *King Lear* and another play, *The Fool*, based upon the life story of John Clare, which certainly does fit the hypotheses of a creative mind being destroyed by the society around it. These are matters for **tragedy**, but this play is **comedy**, the generally harmless folly of unimportant people.

Before considering possible ways of playing comic insanity as depicted by Bond let us consider how other writers show it. Here is an example from a writer who has not only set his action in a private psychiatric clinic, but has as a character a psychiatrist who is obviously mad. In the following extract he is interviewing a pretty girl who is applying to be his secretary. Her conversation cannot be described as being very rational, either.

PRENTICE: Is your mother alive? Or has she too unaccountably vanished? That is a trick question. Be careful – you could lose marks on your final scoring.

[*He returns to his desk and pours himself a whisky*]

GERALDINE: I haven't seen my mother for many years. I was brought up by a Mrs Barclay. She died recently.

PRENTICE: From what cause?

GERALDINE: An explosion, due to a faulty gas-main, killed her outright and took the roof off the house.

PRENTICE: Have you applied for compensation?

GERALDINE: Just for the roof.

PRENTICE: Were there no other victims of the disaster?

GERALDINE: Yes. A recently erected statue of Sir Winston Churchill was so badly injured that the George medal has been talked of. Parts of the great man were actually found embedded in my step-mother.

PRENTICE: Which parts?

GERALDINE: I'm afraid I can't help you there. I was too upset to supervise the funeral arrangements. Or, indeed, to identify the body.

PRENTICE: Surely the Churchill family did that?

GERALDINE: Yes. They were most kind.

PRENTICE: You've had a unique experience. It's not everyone has their step-mother assassinated by the North Thames Gas Board. [*He shakes his head, sharing the poor girl's sorrow*] Can I get you an aspirin?

GERALDINE: No, thank you, sir. I don't want to start taking drugs.

In this play, *What the Butler Saw*, Joe Orton is not making any serious comment upon society, psychiatry or anything else. He is simply exploiting a somewhat corny situation for its possibilities of comic dialogue. Such a scene is best played entirely technically in the manner suitable to **classic farce** such as *The Importance of Being Earnest* (see Chapter Four). In passing, note the complete heartlessness of the situation and dialogue, only permissible in farce.

One way to approach the problem of representing insanity in a comic way upon the stage is to begin by applying a test of rationality. Find out what is possible in any given situation. If you then deliberately choose to attempt the impossible *as if* you thought that it was possible then you would be behaving irrationally. If you persist, then people may think that you are insane. To understand this somewhat abstruse statement, try to perform *The Idiot's Snatch*:

- Grasp the base of your right forefinger with the thumb and fingers of the left hand. To make sure that you have the right grip, hold your hands up together in front of you, so that the right forefinger projects out of the left hand and can be wiggled as if it is bowing at you in a slightly mocking fashion. Do not accept its insolence but decide to catch it with *the right hand* in order to teach it a lesson.

- No sooner do you try to catch it than, by a miracle or perhaps with the assistance of unseen powers, it escapes you! Do not let it get away so easily. Catch it with the left hand and try again.

This game was used a lot in the past as a simple device for portraying comic insanity.

- Now, in pairs, play out an improvisation in which one of the characters is afflicted by a delusion of grandeur. He believes himself to be a person of high rank, great importance or outstanding genius. He completely fails to understand why his very reasonable requests are not immediately granted. He remains polite and well behaved and in every sense of the word *reasonable* apart from his delusions.

- Next, play a scene in which a sane person of some importance finds it difficult to prove his sanity to a sceptic. The circumstances tend to point in the opposite direction. His reasonable explanation may sound mad.

- At this point, discuss how far the test of sanity depends upon what is considered normal in the society applying the test.

- Set up a group improvisation based upon the scene from the ballet of *The Rake's Progress*, in which the highly rational eighteenth-century gentlemen took pleasure in visiting the madhouse on Sundays to observe the obsessions and delusions of the inmates. Also look at the series of pictures by Hogarth from which the ballet was derived.

- The insanity of one person can usually be contained, but suppose a madness becomes, as it were, infectious? Form groups to work out the situation as it might occur when one person with some sort of authority or credibility persuades others to accept his own delusion. Play it first for tragedy and then for comedy.

It is absolutely essential when playing the part of an insane person to avoid all stereotypes and cliches of acting (see Chapter 3.2). A person who is mad does not necessarily distort his limbs, twitch his features, speak thickly, rant, rave or giggle uncontrollably all the time. An insane person may behave reasonably for most of the time, and sane people can behave most unreasonably!

8.4 Characters and relationships

As we have seen, the framework of the play can be worked out in terms of rank and status, set against a pattern of degrees of sanity. This play is set several centuries later than *The Caucasian Chalk Circle*, so the relationships of rank are more subtly expressed. Mrs Rafi is the leader of the Nobs, but Hatch would not like to be called a Peasant. How would he describe himself? And how far are Hollarcut and Thompson on Hatch's side and how far do they owe fealty to Mrs Rafi? (See Chapter 7.2.)

● Consider the characters as falling into groups. Are there any groups outside the two centring round Mrs Rafi and Hatch? What is the difference between the *rank* of Evens and his status? How far does his status differ in the eyes of the two main groups? If he is, as Bond has said, one of the sane characters, what should his status be with the audience?

An actor can approach the creation of his part in several ways. If he has been trained by methods based upon those of Stanislavsky (see Chapter Three), he will consider the character as an *individual*. He will divide the role into small units and consider each unit in turn. He will then look for the motivation of his character. Sometimes, this is called 'finding an objective'. The Brechtian actor will deny that all human actions are psychologically motivated. He will say that most of the things we do arise out of habit formed by influences in society (see Chapter Seven). The theories are not mutually exclusive. Most practising actors have used either method according to the nature of the play in hand.

Like many other writers, Bond works very closely with his actors and their director when a new play is being produced. This makes it very difficult for us to understand the process by which it arrived at the final printed version, which is likely to affect later interpretations. The precision with which Bond describes physical characteristics is unusual and may be inhibiting to later directors. Would you agree that Hatch must necessarily be played by an actor who appears to be '*fortyish, with oiled hair, a rather flat face and very pale blue eyes*'? What other physical characteristics, justified by the text, do you think he could have?

The concept of habitual movement derived from Brecht seems to be useful to us in the early stages of characterisation. Consider the habitual postures of the ladies (refer to Chapter 4.2). They are all gentlefolk, but they vary in age and social position. There are also clues in the play as to the 'pecking-order'. Mrs Rafi is obviously at the top, but in what order are the other ladies? How does this show as they stand, sit or move about in the presence of the others at the rehearsal and, later, at the funeral? Bond adds other character notes. How far is Rose always apart from the ordinary pecking-order? Why should this be?

Habit has also influenced the movements of Hatch. Mad or sane, he is a draper, trained in his craft. He will not be able to play the great tragi-comic scene of the destruction of the curtains with any conviction at all if he cannot wield his scissors as if he has been cutting furnishing fabric for over twenty years.

Bond describes Mrs Tilehouse as *'forties, retiring but determined'*. Can you find similar but equally terse descriptions for the Vicar or Hollarcut or Mafanwy Price or any other character? Mrs Rafi's long speech to Willy in Scene 7 is obviously a fine bravura piece for an actress. So, for an actor, is Hatch's speech in Scene 6 where he tries to kill the already-dead body of Colin.

● Prepare to perform either of these speeches, by going back through the play and picking up all the clues that the writer has planted for you. If you are playing Hatch you should be able to explain the connection between his 'invasion' fantasies, his fear of bankruptcy and his sexual repressions.

8c 'Cutting the curtains'.

Do not forget his inherent dignity as a skilled tradesman. If you are playing Mrs Rafi, consider in what ways she would have been a prisoner of her time and her class. You may think that she shows courage in facing the prospect of lonely old age, but note what Rose says about her after she's gone.

● In a letter quoted in the book mentioned above, Bond says of Evens that he can be excused more easily than other people in the play, but that he could also be condemned more than them. Test this by playing one of his scenes.

8.5 Rehearsing the scene

Scene 4 is the first to be set entirely within Mrs Rafi's territory. Decide where the entrances will be. The position of the windows is critical. There must be space for the rehearsal of Mrs Rafi's play. The round table must be in a position not to distract attention from the important dialogue between Rose and Willy. The disposition of other furniture can be decided later.

● Have available a tape recording of the sea, not as in storm but fairly powerful as if at high tide. Also, if possible, light the scene in a warm colour.

● It will help all the women if they think of such words as 'gentility' 'femininity' 'bereavement' and so on. It might help even more to speak the words aloud in an appropriate tone before actually beginning rehearsal in order to get into the correct mood.

● Now place Rose in the centre of the stage as if she had just entered and compose a tableau around her. Who would be seated? Who stands? Consider the pecking order of the ladies. Where will the Vicar be? Obviously he has some rank, but what is his status in this gathering? Run the tape to a reasonable level so that it will not kill the dialogue, bring up the lights and begin to play the scene.

MRS RAFI: Go back to your room, Rose. We'll manage without you.
ROSE: I'll stay.
MAFANWY: Poor thing.
MRS RAFI: You'll bring yourself down.
ROSE: I can see the sea through the windows.
[*A hushed moan from* LADIES]

This calls for stylised movement, simultaneous, but not in unison.

JILLY: How awful.
MAFANWY: In this town you can't get away from the sea.
MRS RAFI: Pull the curtains.
ROSE: Oh no.
MRS RAFI: The curtains. The curtains. Shut it out.
[LADIES *hurry to close the curtains.*]

Mrs Rafi has now shut out the sea and the sun, so soundtrack and lights are both reduced.

MRS RAFI: Lights.
[LADIES *hurry to fetch lights.*]

Some lighting is restored, but *inside* the room and mainly on Mrs Rafi herself.

The following sequence is very rich comedy but it continues the symbolism. Only the lady of the manor would both produce and play the *male* lead. Later in the scene she identifies herself with God and is very cruel to the faithful and willing Mafanwy Price, who is a very conscientious actress.

● Play the entire scene to bring out the **symbolism**. Then, consider others.

8d   The Rehearsal.

8e   Mrs Rafi.

8.6   Realisation

The first consideration in staging this play must be practicality.

● Make a list of the very large pieces of stage furniture, including the piano, which must be moved on and off.

● Consider also the most strategic places for them to be placed when not in use.

● Now make a list of medium and lightweight furnishings and props.

● Devise a system for rapid striking and setting of the scenes. You may find that you will need the assistance of nearly every member of the cast if you are to manage it quickly, quietly and in darkness.

The Sea *by Edward Bond*

Once you have decided what is practicable, you may then give attention to artistic effects. Obviously the main symbolism will be carried by light and sound.

● Make several tapes of the sound of the sea in a variety of conditions from gale to calm. Consider how and where in the play you would use them.

● Light should be used more in the service of symbolism than of naturalism. Are the shop, house and beach settings indicative of territory? Who dominates each area?

● Obtain illustrations of fashions of the period. Bear in mind that some characters may be old-fashioned for their own times. Suggest modifications according to character and the different ages of the ladies and the various occupations of the men. Willy and Rose are sometimes dressed in white at the end of the play. Is there justification for this?

● Above all, take whatever opportunities occur for the use of colour and general brightness in the design to remind the audience that this is a comedy to be taken seriously but not solemnly.

Glossary

A-EFFECT	(also known as Alienation effect) The means by which Brecht hoped to keep his audiences intellectually and critically interested in the themes within his plays without arousing too much emotional involvement with the characters. To this end, he used non-naturalistic, stylistic settings and trained his actors to play the characters 'from the outside'.
ASIDE	A speech, usually brief, addressed to the audience but by convention not heard by other characters on the stage.
BURLESQUE	A play which makes mockery of any other form of drama. Not the same as SATIRE.
CLASSIC	As applied to literature and drama, this term has two different uses: (1) to categorise all works that are generally recognised as being of outstanding merit; (2) to signify the works of the ancient Greek and Roman writers and those who wrote after them according to classical rules and methods.
COMEDY	The word is derived from the Greek. Nowadays the term is usually taken to apply to any entertaining play with a happy ending.
COMEDY OF CHARACTER	This term could be used to describe most English comedy from Sheridan to the present day. The humour arises from the behaviour of probable although possibly eccentric characters in unusual but not impossible situations.
COMEDY OF HUMOURS	Early-seventeenth-century plays in the style of Jonson, usually highly satirical and with stock characters representative of dominant 'humours' indicated by their names, such as 'Doll Common' or 'Sir Epicure Mammon'.
COMEDY OF MANNERS	Eighteenth-century plays in the style of Congreve and others, in which manners are shown as being absurd and amusing, but little moral judgement or SATIRE is applied.
DIRECT ADDRESS	A form of speech used by an actor, usually in character, to make direct and deliberate communication with the audience.

128

Glossary

EXPRESSIONISM	The use of abstract characters and symbolic action.
FARCE	A kind of comedy in which characters and situations are highly improbable. The entertainment rests entirely on the skill of the performers.
IAMBIC PENTAMETER	The English dramatic metre used by Shakespeare. Each line has five feet, each of two syllables, stressed on the last. Shakespeare himself tended to ignore the rules of prosody.
NATURALISM	The attempt to depict real life in speech and behaviour.
ROMANTIC	This term has many uses, of which the two most important are: (1) to categorise those works of literature and drama dealing with themes of love and adventure and depicting characters motivated by intense emotions, sometimes to an extravagant degree; (2) in a particular sense, the products of the Romantic Movement in art, literature and music in Europe in the early nineteenth century. The movement was a conscious revolt against Classicism.
RESTORATION COMEDY	Late-seventeenth-century plays with outspoken bawdy humour, written to entertain the court of Charles II.
SATIRE	Drama or literature which mocks certain aspects of society. Moral judgement is usually implied.
SOLILOQUY	A speech, usually of some length, spoken in character in order to be 'overheard' by the audience so that they are able to share the thoughts and feelings of the character.
STYLISATION	A deliberate exaggeration of movement or speech designed to achieve a special effect.
SYMBOLISM	A style of writing in which characters, situations and settings are intended to express more than they represent.
THEME	The general idea underlying a play, as distinct from plot or story line.
TRAGEDY	Whether Greek, Roman, Renaissance or modern, depicts a human character as the victim, not of mere misfortune, but of fate. The central character has many noble attributes but his downfall is caused by a 'fatal flaw' in his nature. The writing may be in prose or verse, but is usually elevated in style. The Greek philosopher Aristotle held that the audience at a tragedy were purged of their own evil tendencies by the contemplation of pitiful and terrible events.

Booklist

Clive Barker, *Theatre Games* (Methuen, 1977).

John Barton, *RSC in Playing Shakespeare* (Methuen in association with Channel Four, 1984).

Cicely Berry, *Voice and the Actor* (Harrap, 1973).

Brecht on Theatre, ed. J. Willett (Methuen, 1964).

Edward Bond: A Companion to the Plays ed. Malcolm Hay and Philip Roberts (TQ Publications, 1978).

William Hobbs, *Techniques of the Stage Fight* (Studio Vista, 1974).

Lyn Oxenford, *Playing Period Plays* (J. Garnet Miller, 1959).

Philippe Perrottet, *Practical Stage Make-up* (Studio Vista, 1967).

Litz Pisk, *The Actor and His Body* (Harrap, 1975).

Francis Reed, *The Stage Lighting Handbook* (Pitman, 1976).

Theatre At Work, ed. Charles Marowitz and Simon Trussler (Methuen, 1967). (This contains the interview with William Gaskill, 'Brecht in Britain'.)

The Theory of the Modern Stage, ed. Eric Bentley (Penguin, 1968).

K. A. Stanislavsky, *An Actor Prepares* (Geoffrey Bles, 1937).

K. A. Stanislavsky, *Building a Character* (Methuen, 1968).

Raymond Williams, *Drama from Ibsen to Brecht* (Penguin, 1973).

Index

Index

RENNER LEARNING RESOURCE CENTER
ELGIN COMMUNITY COLLEGE
ELGIN, ILLINOIS 60123

RENNER LEARNING RESOURCE CENTER
ELGIN COMMUNITY COLLEGE
ELGIN, ILLINOIS 60123